60 AMERICAN HEROES

EVERY KID SHOULD MEET

To my wonderful family and friends, all of whom have enriched my life —D.D.

To all the strong women in my life, who inspire me and give me courage —L.R.

Thank you to the people who helped bring this book to fruition:

Byron Hollinshead

Jon M. Fishman

Elizabeth McPike

Dr. Harold Robles

Thank you to the people who aided our research process:

Kevin Williams

Diana and Don Durand

Richard Yednock

Susan Miller

Charlie Welch

Stephan Williams

Julianne Dickson

Helene Guilfoy

Jane Addams Hull House Association

Stephen Miller, DDS

George C. Marshall Foundation

Helen Keller National Center (HKNC) for DeafBlind Youth and Adults

Tura Campanella-Cook of the Jane Addams Peace Association

Supreme Court of the United States, Public Information Office

The dedicated librarians at Millersville University's Ganser Library and the Lancaster County Library

Thanks to Jason Redcay, Jonathon Ober, and Nate Martin for their help with the Vote for Your Hero contest

Thanks to Michael G. Roscoe, and Allison and Bethany Roscoe for their continuing patience and support

Thank you also to teachers John Mohn, Georgette Hackman, Amy Evans, and Dr. Cole Reilly

And a special thank-you to Angie Post-Speitel for crusading to include her hero, Mary McLeod Bethune, in this book

Millbrook Press
An imprint of Lerner Publishing Group, Inc.
241 First Avenue North
Minneapolis, MN 55401 USA

For reading levels and more information, look up this title at www.lernerbooks.com.

Main body text set in Chaparral Pro Regular 12/15.
Typeface provided by Adobe Systems.

Library of Congress Cataloging-in-Publication Data

Names: Denenberg, Dennis, 1947– author. | Roscoe, Lorraine, 1955– author.
Title: 60 American heroes every kid should meet / by Dennis Denenberg, Lorraine Roscoe.
Other titles: Sixty American heroes every kid should meet
Description: Minneapolis : Millbrook Press, [2023] | Includes bibliographical references and index. | Audience: Ages 11–18 | Audience: Grades 7–9 | Summary: "Encounter sixty remarkable Americans and their inspiring stories in browseable, photo-illustrated pages. Revised by the original authors, this unique book includes up-to-date websites, book lists, and biographical information"— Provided by publisher.
Identifiers: LCCN 2021052297 (print) | LCCN 2021052298 (ebook) | ISBN 9781728449302 (library binding) | ISBN 9781728449319 (paperback) | ISBN 9781728460505 (ebook)
Subjects: LCSH: Heroes—United States—Biography—Juvenile literature. | United States—Biography—Juvenile literature.
Classification: LCC CT217 .D464 2023 (print) | LCC CT217 (ebook) | DDC 920.073—dc23/eng/20211029

LC record available at https://lccn.loc.gov/2021052297
LC ebook record available at https://lccn.loc.gov/2021052298

Manufactured in the United States of America
1-50431-49940-3/7/2022

60 AMERICAN HEROES

EVERY KID SHOULD MEET

DENNIS DENENBERG AND LORRAINE ROSCOE

M MILLBROOK PRESS · MINNEAPOLIS

CONTENTS

A TRIBUTE

In the introduction on pages 8–9, we challenge you to name sixty important American heroes. We think you will name some people we don't know, or who wouldn't have occurred to us. But they are heroes to you, and that's very important.

All of us have personal heroes. They are the people in our lives who have helped to shape our personalities and define who we are. Often we don't even realize how important and special they are.

Maybe the closest members of your family are personal heroes. Think about how much they have helped you. Sure, there are times you have disagreed with their advice or actions, but they have been there for you when you needed them.

How about teachers? Religious leaders? Doctors? Coaches? Club leaders? Your friends' parents? Even your siblings—yes, they can be your personal heroes too!

Do you ever thank your personal heroes? Telling someone they are your personal hero is different from telling them you love them. That's important too, but letting them know that they are your hero is a powerful way of thanking them.

The United States is full of heroes. They often don't get the credit they deserve, so we sometimes refer to them as unsung heroes. They are the firefighters who rush into burning buildings to save people and pets, the police officers who risk their lives to keep us safe, and the protesters and activists who work to make the world better and more fair. Heroes serve in our armed forces to keep the country free, create art and music to bring beauty to our lives, and inspire us with their athletic achievements, and work to level the playing field for all competitors.

Heroes do what it takes to make this world a better place. We want you to think about the importance of the heroes in your life, and we hope you'll take some action to let them know how special they are to you.

INTRODUCTION

How quickly can you name 60 American heroes? They can be young or old, from the past or present, living or dead, and any gender, but they *all* must have made an exceptional positive contribution to our world.

How'd you do? Were you able to come up with 60 names? Who's on your list? Chances are, a few names popped right up: George Washington, Abraham Lincoln, Martin Luther King Jr. Then maybe you mentioned people you are studying in school, such as Thomas Jefferson, Eleanor Roosevelt, or Harriet Tubman. After that, perhaps you listed a few important people in the news—Jimmy Carter, Dr. Anthony Fauci, even Oprah Winfrey. But you *still* didn't have 60 names, so you moved on to sports stars, rock singers, and other celebrities who may or may not deserve to be called heroes. Maybe you even filled out your list with imaginary heroes, such as your favorite TV or movie characters.

Coming up with a list of 60 wasn't easy, was it?

We didn't think so either, and that's why we wrote this book. Every kid needs great people to admire and imitate, but how can you look up to them if you don't know who they are?

Among our heroes are architects and aviators, activists and scientists, entrepreneurs and advocates. They are teachers, musicians, inventors, and athletes. Some are well known. Others *deserve* to be. Some of our heroes lived long ago. Others continue to enrich our world today. Our heroes share admirable qualities: exceptional talent, fierce determination, and indomitable spirit. They are courageous and confident and possess an unwavering commitment to being the best they can be.

Can only an American be a hero? Of course not. But America is like no other place in the world. Here, heroes can be rich or poor, young or old, and of any race, religion, or national origin under the sun. The opportunities open to us are almost endless. We're free to follow any dream that enters our heads, and we have every right to expect fair treatment from others as we do so. It's as simple as that.

Our goal is to provide you with a launching pad to discover new heroes. Then you can have fun learning more as you decide which heroes interest you the most.

So what do these 60 American heroes have to do with you? Everything. They might be what you want to be when you grow up. Although their shoes may seem impossible to fill, you'll find that many of our heroes were a lot like you when they were young. They had families, homes, classmates, part-time jobs. Many had doubts about their own abilities to make a difference in this world.

Read about them. Hear their stories. We've given you a few good books to get you started on finding out more about each of our heroes. Heroes usually seem larger than life. They are so great as to seem almost unreal to us. But all of them are *real* people. Reading their biographies can help you learn more about their childhoods, their friends and families, their hobbies, and all the other things that make them just like you.

Because they are real people, these heroes are not perfect. Sometimes they made dreadful choices and did things that harmed others. Some of our greatest heroes—our country's founders—made the terrible decision to enslave others. While we wish our heroes always did everything perfectly, they are real people who can make serious mistakes.

To add a little action to your search for heroes, we've included a number of activities in this book. We give you lots of places—museums, foundations, national parks—to contact. Website addresses are listed, or you can just search online and check out the always growing list of links to your favorite heroes.

You'll have a great time exploring new ideas, and you won't be alone. As you explore this book, you'll see that we have made it possible for you to interact with us, the authors.

Are our heroes the *only* ones you need to know about? No way! We can name hundreds more people who have done great things. In fact, we want you to find more heroes using our Hero Hunt. On page 134, we give you clues about individuals similar to the featured heroes. It's up to you to solve the mysteries of who they are. The answers are listed on page 142, but please, NO PEEKING until you have done some digging.

If you believe that some of *your* heroes should have made our list of 60, we would like to hear from you. Perhaps you know of an accomplished ballet dancer, a brilliant scientist, or a courageous humanitarian that was not on our roster of heroes. Or maybe you admire your grandfather, your teacher, or even an exceptional member of your church, synagogue, mosque, or other house of worship. Contact us and tell us why you hold them in such high regard. Better yet, tell your *friends* who your heroes are. The people you look up to can change other kids' lives too. If you're willing to spread the word. Here's our website: www.heroes4us.com.

It's time for real heroes.

JANE ADDAMS

THE FIRST LADY OF PEACE
HUMANITARIAN
AUTHOR
NOBEL PEACE PRIZE WINNER

You've probably heard of Mother Teresa, the Roman Catholic nun who devoted her life to helping the world's poor people. But did you know that more than one hundred years ago, an American-born woman did the same? Her name was Jane Addams, and she almost always knew that she wanted to help people.

Jane Addams was a woman of action! In Europe she learned of a program in which educated young men moved into a poor section of London and offered classes and activities to people right there in the neighborhood. She thought it was such a great idea that she brought it home and founded Hull House in Chicago.

In a huge mansion, surrounded by the crowded homes of poor people, Jane Addams and her friends created a haven. There, they taught their neighbors job skills, cared for their children, started a kindergarten, and formed a boys' club (which called itself the Young Heroes Club). Food, friendship, financial help—you could find them all at Hull House.

Jane Addams saw it all very simply: neighbors helping neighbors.

In 1979 Mother Teresa (an honorary US citizen) won the Nobel Peace Prize. She followed in the footsteps of the first American woman ever to be awarded that prize—Jane Addams.

Jane Addams posed for this photograph in 1914. She supported reforms benefiting children such as the first state child labor law and the first juvenile court.

EXPLORE!
Another cause that got Jane Addams moving and called her to action was world peace. She was the founder and first president of the Women's International League for Peace and Freedom (WILPF). Just as she worked hard at Hull House to help the poor, she worked hard to promote world harmony.

Because Jane also wrote numerous books, each year the Jane Addams Children's Book

"Action indeed is the sole medium of expression for ethics. [Ethics is knowing right from wrong.]"

—Jane Addams

Awards honors children's books that promote peace and social justice. We think you will find these books to be great reading. Some of the award-winning books are biographies of heroes, some are stories of young people struggling for freedom, and many are stories of incredible courage. If you would like to read about the events and people who stand for the same values of peace and community that Jane Addams stood for, visit www.janeaddamschildrensbookaward.org.

EXPLORE SOME MORE!

Pay a virtual visit to the Jane Addams Hull-House Museum at www.hullhousemuseum.org.

DIVE IN!

Jane Addams: Champion of Democracy by Judith Blood Fradin and Dennis Brindell Fradin (Clarion Books, 2006), 216 pages.

Jane Addams interacts with children at Hull House around 1930.

SUSAN B. ANTHONY

FEBRUARY 15, 1820–MARCH 13, 1906

CHAMPION FOR WOMEN'S RIGHTS
SUFFRAGETTE (A WOMAN WHO ADVOCATES THE RIGHT TO VOTE FOR WOMEN)
VISIONARY
AUTHOR

"Men and Boys Only." "No Females Allowed." Can you imagine signs like that posted at your favorite store? Your favorite fast-food restaurant? How would it make you feel? Now imagine that sign on college applications, on certain careers such as medicine and the law. ON VOTING BOOTHS!

At one time, American women didn't have to imagine any of this. For them, it was real. They were not allowed to do a lot of things that men were allowed to do. And sometimes, they could even be arrested for trying.

Susan B. Anthony came from a Quaker heritage that believed in the equality of men and women— but most Americans at the time, especially men, did not agree.

On November 5, 1872, Susan B. Anthony broke the law. So did fifteen other women. Eventually, they were all placed under arrest, as were the three men who had allowed them to break the law. The scandal made headlines in newspapers across the country.

What horrible crime had Susan B. Anthony committed? She and fifteen of her friends had voted. They just walked into a polling place and cast their ballots—and in most places in the United States that was against the law.

In the trial that followed many months later, the judge made a mockery of justice. Anthony was the only one of the sixteen women put on trial, and the judge found her guilty and fined her $100 (she never paid it).

The three men who let her vote were also found guilty and spent five days in jail.

All this because a woman *voted*!

What did the whole incident prove? Sadly, it showed how women were treated like second-class citizens. Susan B. Anthony couldn't vote or receive a fair trial. Many of the men in our country wanted to keep all the power and not share it with women.

Unfortunately, she didn't live to see her dream fulfilled, but many of her fellow suffragettes did. In August 1920, the Nineteenth Amendment to the US Constitution was ratified, and women became first-class citizens. Finally, women were among "we, the people," allowed to take an active part in our democracy. The amendment guaranteed women the right to vote, but Black women were still barred from voting in many parts of the country until the 1965 Voting Rights Act.

"It was we, the people; not we, the white male citizens; nor yet we, the male citizens; but we, the whole people, who formed the Union." —*Susan B. Anthony*

Thanks to the years of work of Susan B. Anthony, all females can cast a ballot when they reach eighteen. Don't take it for granted.

EXPLORE

Seneca Falls, New York, is the home of the National Women's Hall of Fame. Visit www.womenofthehall.org to explore it online.

You'll learn

- why it's located in Seneca Falls
- who, besides Susan B. Anthony, were other famous suffragettes
- what actions they took to get the vote for women

In the introduction to this book, we asked you to help us come up with the next list of 60 heroes. Now's your chance! Find out about the other women and what they did to qualify for this great honor. Visit the Hall of Fame website and click on "Women of the Hall." By clicking on individual photos of Hall of Famers, you can learn a little or a lot more about these amazing role models.

Choose someone who has interests similar to yours and read their biography. Did we include them in this book? Do they belong in the next one? State your case!

Okay, maybe you're saying "What about a Hall of Fame for men?" Good question. Should we start one? Where would it be? Who should be in it? There are many men's sports halls of fame (football, baseball, golf, basketball, etc.). But what about a Hall of Fame for great men in any field? Should the Women's Hall of Fame be open to men? Is admittance to a Hall of Fame based on gender a sexist idea? Good topic for a blog post!

DIVE IN!

Elizabeth Cady Stanton and Susan B. Anthony: A Friendship That Changed the World by Penny Colman (Henry Holt, 2011), 256 pages.

In 1869 Susan B. Anthony *(right)* and her friend and fellow woman's rights leader Elizabeth Cady Stanton *(left)* founded the National Woman Suffrage Association to work for a woman suffrage amendment to the Constitution. Find out more about the group at http://www.crusadeforthevote.org/nwsa-organize.

CLARA BARTON

ANGEL OF THE BATTLEFIELD
NURSE
HUMANITARIAN
FOUNDER, AMERICAN RED CROSS
AUTHOR

September 17, 1862, is called the bloodiest day of the American Civil War (1861–1865).

It was the day of the Battle of Antietam (some call it the Battle of Sharpsburg), and Clara Barton was there to help care for the wounded. As cannon shells exploded and male nurses ran for cover, she stayed by the surgeon's side, steadying the crude operating table. He later called her "the true heroine of the age, the angel of the battlefield."

Clara Barton posed for this portrait around the year 1860, just before the Civil War.

She knew she had to go. The United States' worst flood disaster ever had devastated Johnstown, Pennsylvania. A dam had burst, sending a raging river into the mining town. In just four hours, floodwaters had killed more than two thousand people. Those left behind needed help. They needed Clara Barton and her organization, the American Red Cross.

The year was 1889. Clara spent four months in Johnstown helping the survivors, never once leaving the scene, even for a day. Working from giant tents, she directed hundreds of volunteers in distributing blankets, food, clothes, and money. Flying above her command tent was the red-and-white flag that is now recognized everywhere in the United States and around the world—the Red Cross flag.

But before the guiding force behind that flag became so famous, she was a shy, withdrawn little girl from a small town in Massachusetts. Clara had always loved helping people. When she was eleven, her brother David fell from a barn roof and was badly hurt. Young Clara would be his nurse. During the next two years, Clara left his bedside for only one-half hour a day!

Nearly thirty years later, Clara Barton would spend day and night caring for the wounded and dying soldiers of the Union army during the American Civil War. She offered her tender care to everyone—Northern soldiers, Southern prisoners of war, white men, and Black men.

After the war, she headed the government's search for missing soldiers. She became one of the United States' most beloved heroes. For the remainder of her life after the Civil War, she continued her humanitarian work and built the organization we know as the American Red Cross.

"[I pledge] before God all that I have, all that I am, all that I can, and all that I hope to be, to the cause of justice and mercy, and patriotism, my country and my God." —*Clara Barton*

EXPLORE!

Its headquarters is a stone's throw from the White House in Washington, DC. Clara Barton's Red Cross building stands as a sturdy symbol of the organization's commitment to lend a hand whenever and wherever disaster strikes. In the midst of earthquakes, floods, acts of terrorism, fires, tornadoes, volcanic eruptions, hurricanes, or any other catastrophe, Red Cross volunteers are always there to help. Why? Because they have the same caring spirit as Clara Barton. One of the United States' strengths has always been its people's willingness to help those whose lives

DIVE IN!

Clara Barton's Civil War: Between Bullet and Hospital by Donald Pfanz (Westholme Publishing, 2018), 228 pages.

are shattered by disaster. Visit www.redcross.org to learn how the Red Cross is making a difference where you live.

EXPLORE SOME MORE!

What about you? Do you want to pitch in? Kids That Do Good was created by kids to connect young people with ways to give back. Check it out at www.kidsthatdogood.com. Find out what kinds of things kids your age are doing to help out in their neighborhoods. Volunteering is the best gift you can offer your community, and it makes you feel pretty good too.

Clara Barton (*center in red cape*) is shown here tending to wounded soldiers during the Civil War. Barton's nursing and administrative skills caused her to be present during many famous events in American history.

MARY MCLEOD BETHUNE

PIONEER FOR EQUAL RIGHTS
EDUCATOR
HUMANITARIAN
CIVIL RIGHTS ACTIVIST

More than anything, Mary McLeod Bethune knew that education gives you the power to change your life. Why? Because the opportunity to go to school changed hers.

In Mayesville, South Carolina, Mary began her formal education when she was eleven years old. She was the fifteenth of seventeen children of formerly enslaved people. Many of her older siblings had also been born into slavery. Like them, she worked as a child in the cotton fields on her parents' homestead. But something deep inside of Mary—a passion, a spirit, a hunger—drove her to look for more. Mary wanted to learn and teach and lead. So, in a one-room schoolhouse, with Emma Jane Wilson as her teacher, Mary's new life began.

It's not surprising then that Mary felt so strongly about "giving back" the gift of learning. In 1904, with only $1.50, she opened the Daytona (Florida) Literary and Industrial School for Training Negro Girls. There were only six students (five girls and Mary's son) in this elementary school, but over the next twenty-five years, it grew steadily, transforming into a high school, junior college, and finally Bethune-Cookman University. The story of its survival and growth will forever be the greatest tribute to Mary's determination and energy.

An appointee of President Franklin D. Roosevelt, Mary McLeod Bethune served as director of the Division of Negro Affairs of the National Youth Administration from 1936 to 1944.

She channeled her energy into other efforts too. She started a hospital for Black people when she saw how discrimination prevented proper medical care. She became a national spokesperson for the rights of African Americans prior to our country's dramatic civil rights movement. She even faced eighty white-hooded Ku Klux Klansmen and forced them to retreat over the issue of Black people having the right to vote. For more than twenty-five years, this human dynamo moved forward with determination, educating, organizing, even advising presidents. She encouraged Black people, particularly women, to step forward with confidence and dignity and make their voices heard.

EXPLORE!

Over the entrance to a Bethune-Cookman building are the words "Enter to Learn." As you leave the building, you see the words, "Depart to Serve."

She wanted her legacy to reach far beyond the walls of the organizations that she had founded. She wanted to spread the "principles and policies" in which she firmly believed. "I will pass them on to Negroes everywhere," she wrote, "in the hope that an old woman's philosophy may give them inspiration."

Read Mary's *My Last Will and Testament.* Her words will inspire and encourage you. Find it at https://www.cookman.edu/history/last-will-testament.html. What do her words mean to you as a young person? Make a copy of the document and save it. Then read it again in five years. In ten years. In twenty-five years. See if its meaning for you changes as you get older.

DIVE IN!

Mary McLeod Bethune in Florida: Bringing Social Justice to the Sunshine State by Ashley N. Robertson (Arcadia Press, 2015), 144 pages.

EXPLORE SOME MORE!

There's a great statue of Mary McLeod Bethune in Washington, DC. It's the first monument to honor a Black woman in a public park in Washington. Search online to see the statue for yourself. A new statue of Mary McLeod Bethune is planned for the nation's capital in 2022. It will represent Florida at the US Capitol's National Statuary Hall. If you can, stop by to check it out!

Mary McLeod Bethune *(left)* awards prizes to high-achieving students at a ceremony in Washington, DC, in 1939.

POWER WORDS!

"I leave you love. . . . I leave you hope. . . . I leave you the challenge of developing confidence in one another. . . . I leave you a thirst for education. . . . I leave you respect for the uses of power. . . . I leave you faith. . . . I leave you racial dignity. . . . I leave you a desire to live harmoniously with your fellow men. . . . I leave you finally a responsibility to our young people."

—*Mary McLeod Bethune,* My Last Will and Testament

ELIZABETH BLACKWELL

FEBRUARY 3, 1821–MAY 31, 1910

FIRST AMERICAN WOMAN DOCTOR

PHYSICIAN
HUMANITARIAN
TRAILBLAZER
AUTHOR

There's nothing unusual about a female doctor. But not so long ago, a lot of people thought the idea was ridiculous.

Even when she was young, Elizabeth Blackwell was strong-willed and stubborn, not reserved and submissive like girls were expected to be.

But not even young Elizabeth considered studying medicine. Not until a dying friend planted the seed. Her sick neighbor appreciated the hours that Elizabeth spent taking care of her. "If I could have been treated by a lady doctor, my worst sufferings would have been spared me," she said. "If only *you* were a doctor."

Elizabeth a doctor? Well, why not? It was a path no woman had ever attempted to follow. Medical schools were for men only, so Elizabeth Blackwell spent years preparing with the help of some friendly doctors before she even applied. She wanted to be ready to succeed.

She was twenty-five when she began to apply to medical schools. She collected rejection after rejection—from all of them. More rejection letters came, bringing the total to twenty-eight. How would you feel? Would you give up?

Then the letter from Geneva Medical College in New York arrived. *Acceptance!* She

This portrait of Elizabeth Blackwell was created in approximately 1850.

was finally on the road to earning her medical degree. Only upon arriving at the college did she learn why she was accepted. It was a joke! The school's faculty had not wanted her, but in order to avoid making that decision, they asked the all-male student body to vote. The men voted unanimously for her entry. They figured some other medical school was playing a practical joke. But the joke was on them. The Geneva faculty had to honor the vote, and Elizabeth Blackwell was in.

And she had the last laugh. After the two-year program was over, Dr. Elizabeth

"For what is done or learned by one class of women becomes, by virtue of their common womanhood, the property of all women." —*Elizabeth Blackwell*

Blackwell graduated number one in her class. The struggle had been long and lonely, but she made it. She was a doctor.

However, Dr. Blackwell did not then coast on to fame and fortune. After all, she had to convince patients to allow themselves to be *examined* by a female doctor! What followed was a roller-coaster life of accomplishment and disappointment. She would need every ounce of her intelligence, determination, and independent spirit to make it work. Do you think she did it? Do you think

DIVE IN!

Elizabeth Blackwell: Trailblazing Woman Doctor by Matt Doeden (Lerner Publications, 2022), 48 pages.

we would have included her in this book if she didn't?

EXPLORE!

Dr. Blackwell dedicated her life to curing people. How much do you know about first aid? Could you help a friend who suddenly was injured? Would you know what simple things to do and not to do? You can be ready to help a family member or friend by learning CPR, mouth-to-mouth resuscitation, the Heimlich maneuver, and other first-aid techniques. By staying calm and acting responsibly, you might be able to save a life until the 911 emergency squad arrives.

How do you get this information? First, check with your school nurse or health and physical education teachers. The American Red Cross, scouting groups, and youth organizations all provide training. The website for the American Red Cross is www.redcross.org. This informative site will pinpoint the Red Cross instruction location closest to your home.

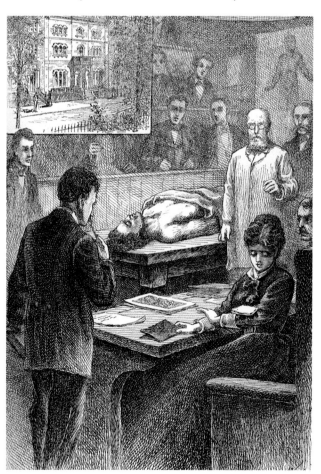

Although her fellow medical students voted her into the school as a joke, Blackwell earned their respect. Her only real problem was being the only female in the class on human reproduction. She later recalled: "Some of the students blushed, some were hysterical. . . . I had to pinch my hand till the blood nearly came . . . to keep me from smiling."

RACHEL CARSON

"A SOLITARY CHILD"
ENVIRONMENTALIST
AUTHOR

Rachel Carson called herself "a solitary child." She loved to spend "a great deal of time in woods and beside streams, learning the birds and the insects and flowers." Being out in nature made her feel good about herself. She also fell in love with reading and writing when she was very young. Those interests—nature, reading, and writing—would one day make young Rachel Carson a famous crusader.

St. Nicholas was a magazine for kids. In fact, it was the most popular children's magazine when Rachel Carson was a ten-year-old growing up in Springdale, Pennsylvania. This magazine asked its readers to submit poems, stories, and drawings for publication. If you got published, you got paid. When she was ten, Rachel sold a story to *St. Nicholas*, and they paid her ten dollars. This was the beginning of Rachel's professional writing career.

Later in life, Rachel Carson would combine her love of nature with her love and talent for writing. Mostly she wrote about ecology, conservation, and the environment. These are things we talk about all the time, but in her day, people thought only scientists needed to know about such things. They didn't realize how precious our environment is and how we have to work together to protect it.

Rachel Carson helped change all that. She was a courageous as well as a talented writer. In her last book, *Silent Spring*, she challenged many wealthy and influential people in business

Rachel Carson loved nature her entire life.

POWER WORDS!

"In nature, nothing exists alone."

—*Rachel Carson*, Silent Spring

and government by telling the world how the use of pesticides was poisoning the planet. Her opponents ridiculed her, but others listened and learned. Thanks to her brave words, the food we eat is no longer contaminated with the dangerous pesticide called DDT.

EXPLORE!

Freedom of the press is guaranteed under our Bill of Rights (the US Constitution's first ten amendments). It means that writers can write about almost anything, as long as they tell the truth.

Rachel Carson saw a wrong and tried to right it by using the power of the freedom of the press in writing about it. You can do the same! Maybe there's a dangerous intersection in your town or neighborhood that needs a traffic light or stop sign to be made safe. Maybe classrooms in your school are overcrowded. Maybe you know about a place where people are dumping trash illegally. You can try to change things.

Search online for publications or blogs that want to hear from readers. Your local newspaper, a magazine, and even corporate or nonprofit newsletters are likely candidates. Organize your thoughts and let your passion for a cause shine through. Don't forget to offer solutions to the problem! Your willingness to step forward may catch the attention of others interested in the same issues. Who knows what will happen next?

The success of *Silent Spring* made Rachel Carson a well-known voice on environmental issues. Here she speaks before a United States Senate subcommittee in 1963 about the dangers of pesticides and other chemicals.

EXPLORE SOME MORE!

Contact the Rachel Carson Council for more information on current efforts to fight toxic and chemical threats to our environment:

Rachel Carson Council
https://www.rachelcarsoncouncil.org

Some other organizations concerned with preserving our planet are

The Life and Legacy of Rachel Carson
https://www.rachelcarson.org

National Wildlife Federation
https://www.nwf.org

US Environmental Protection Agency
https://www.epa.gov

DIVE IN!

Rachel Carson by Anita Croy
(Crabtree, 2021), 64 pages.

Also, please read *Silent Spring*. Then you'll see firsthand how powerful Rachel Carson's words really are.

JIMMY CARTER

OCTOBER 1, 1924–

PEACEMAKER
US PRESIDENT
HUMANITARIAN
NOBEL PEACE PRIZE WINNER
AUTHOR

Only in America could a peanut farmer named Jimmy become president of the United States and remain a statesman respected around the world.

Camp David is our presidents' vacation home. In 1978 President Jimmy Carter brought two extraordinary world leaders to Camp David: Anwar Sadat, the president of Egypt, and Menachem Begin, the prime minister of Israel. These two Middle Eastern countries had been at war for more than thirty years. Many people, including children, had been killed in battle and by acts of terrorism. But Jimmy Carter believed that if he could get Sadat and Begin to talk face-to-face, they could begin to work out their problems.

One of the simple things our president did that kept the peace talks going was to autograph some photos. The Israeli leader had requested autographed pictures of the three men together. He wanted them for his grandchildren. Well, President Carter had his secretary find out the names of these special kids and he personalized each photo. When Begin was handed the pictures, he politely thanked the president. Then he looked at the autographs and read their names. His grandchildren's names. The tough old leader's

Since his four years as president of the United States (1977–1981), Jimmy Carter has worked with Habitat for Humanity, an organization that builds simple, affordable housing in partnership with people in need. Kids can also help, so look into it at www.habitat.org.

POWER WORDS!

"I do what I do because I think it is the right thing to do." —*Jimmy Carter*

eyes filled with tears. The sight of those names led him to talk about those special people in his life and about the terrible effects of war on children. Dramatically, the tone of the talks turned around—and a settlement was reached. In 2002 President Carter was awarded the Nobel Prize for Peace.

EXPLORE!

President Carter lost his reelection campaign in 1980. Sometimes, ex-presidents don't quite know what to do, but not Jimmy Carter. He has been one of our busiest former chief executives. And he has become one of the most respected and recognized Americans in the world. That's because he has devoted his time and energy to peacemaking missions around the globe. He's been all over the planet working for peace, human rights, and democracy—in Bosnia, Panama, Nicaragua, Haiti, Nigeria, Ethiopia, North and South Korea, and in the Middle East.

You can find out more about these efforts and what Jimmy Carter is currently doing by visiting the Carter Center's website at www.cartercenter.org.

You can also explore the Jimmy Carter Presidential Library and Museum and learn more about Jimmy Carter's extraordinary life at https://www.jimmycarterlibrary.gov/about_us /biography_of_jimmy_carter.

EXPLORE SOME MORE!

Jimmy Carter and his wife, Rosalynn Carter, have devoted countless hours to Habitat for Humanity. Check out the nonprofit organization's story, and contact your local Habitat for Humanity chapter to see how you can get involved: https://www.habitat .org/volunteer/build-events /carter-work-project.

DIVE IN!

James Earl Carter by Lori Hobkirk (Child's World, 2020), 48 pages.

Jimmy Carter wears a tool belt and a hard hat on the site of a Habitat for Humanity project in San Pedro, California, in 2007.

GEORGE WASHINGTON CARVER

CA. 1864–JANUARY 5, 1943

THE REAL MR. PEANUT

EDUCATOR
PLANT SCIENTIST
AGRICULTURE INNOVATOR
AUTHOR

George Washington Carver once told a story about a conversation he had with God. He asked God to tell him the mystery of the universe. God replied that George was asking about something much too grand. Then George asked God to tell him all about the peanut. And God decided that the peanut was much more nearly George's size. So God showed George what the peanut was all about.

The next time you gobble up a peanut butter and jelly sandwich, think of George Washington Carver. He turned the humble peanut into an agricultural giant.

What got him interested in peanuts? It all started with an insect. In the late 1800s, cotton was the major cash crop for farmers in the southern states. But the dreaded Mexican boll weevil was threatening to eat the plants and destroy the farmers' income. Besides, all that cotton growing was wearing out the land. The farmers needed a change. Farmers, however, were scared to switch. They knew how to raise cotton, and they knew cotton would sell. Carver realized that if he were to get farmers to change their habits, he had to prove to them that some other

A portrait of George Washington Carver taken around the year 1906

crop would be just as valuable as cotton.

Experimenting, he came up with more than three hundred ways to use peanuts. There were dyes, fruit punches (cherry, lemon, and orange), milk, facial cream, ink, relish, and even a peanut curd that tasted just like meat. Carver had proven that peanuts had potential.

This great scientist had always been interested in plants and insects even when he was a boy. But learning about the natural world around him was not easy. He was born into slavery and battled terrible discrimination against Black people his entire life. Yet, George Washington Carver was determined to succeed, and succeed he did. He became a gifted and respected botanist.

POWER WORDS!

"It has always been the one great ideal of my life to be of the greatest good to the greatest number of 'my people' possible, and to this end I have been preparing myself for these many years; feeling as I do that this line of education is the key to unlock the golden door of freedom to our people."

—*George Washington Carver*

DIVE IN!

A Pocketful of Goobers: A Story about George Washington Carver by Barbara Mitchell (Millbrook Press, 1986), 64 pages.

He was invited to be a professor at Tuskegee Institute in Alabama. After his death, the US Congress paid tribute to him by dedicating his birthplace site near Diamond, Missouri, as a national monument. President Franklin D. Roosevelt said of George Washington Carver: "The things which he achieved in the face of early handicaps will for all time afford an inspiring example to youth everywhere."

EXPLORE!

The United States has often been called "the land of opportunity" because people of any color, religion, or ethnic background can be successful. We are free to follow our dreams, just as the "peanut doctor" did.

Scientists often use their imaginations when they pursue their dreams. They try to come up with new ways to look at concepts, objects, and facts, like Professor Carver did with the peanut. Your task is to take a common natural product (like a potato or a daisy or a dog hair) and become Professor Carver. Design new ways for that product to be used. Let your imagination run wild. If you can, test your new ideas to see if they work. Visit https://www.livescience.com/47642-discoveries-by-kids.html to read "7 Awesome Discoveries Made by Kids." Yours may be number eight! Great things can happen when thinkers like you play with the impossible.

The depth of commitment to his research was made clear when Carver donated his entire life savings of $33,000 to Tuskegee Institute (*left*) to establish a fund to carry on the agricultural and chemical work he began.

CESAR CHAVEZ AND DOLORES HUERTA

CHAVEZ: MARCH 31, 1927–APRIL 23, 1993

HUERTA: APRIL 10, 1930–

CHAMPIONS OF THE MIGRANT WORKERS
LABOR LEADERS
CIVIL RIGHTS ACTIVISTS

Dolores Huerta (*left*) and Cesar Chavez (*center*) in 1968. Chavez was near the end of a twenty-five-day hunger strike to support United Farm Workers of America.

Those of you who have moved **know that means change.** It means giving up some things you like. It means learning and adapting. Now imagine young Cesar's life. By the time he was in the eighth grade, he had attended more than three dozen different schools! Why? Because his family members were migrant workers.

Migrant workers are the hardworking people who harvest many of the fruits and vegetables we eat. While machines can help, adults and children still pick the crops. Migrant workers settle wherever there's produce to pick, then move on when the work is done.

Living conditions for migrant farmworkers were awful. In the 1960s they were making a dollar an hour for long workdays. They traveled in rickety trucks and buses to fields sprayed with pesticide poisons. Their homes were crowded, dismal shacks without electricity or running water.

Migrant workers had no money, no power, and no voice. When Cesar grew up, he became their voice, as did Dolores Huerta. Teamwork brought them together, and they started the organization known as the United Farm Workers of America (visit their website at https://ufw.org). By using labor strikes and boycotts, Cesar Chavez and Dolores Huerta made Americans aware of just how bad conditions were for migrant workers.

Together they led peaceful protests, made speeches, and started the Boycott Grapes campaign. The country paid attention to this team. We stopped eating grapes and drinking wine from nonworker-friendly vineyards. The growers paid attention, and life improved for migrant farmworkers.

POWER WORDS!

"Students must have initiative; they should not be mere imitators. They must learn to think and act for themselves and be free." —*Cesar Chavez*

"I would like to be remembered as a woman who cares for fellow humans. We must use our lives to make the world a better place to live, not just to acquire things. That is what we are put on the earth for." —*Dolores Huerta*

EXPLORE!

Sometimes, if we don't hear anything about a problem for a while, we think it's solved. How about the migrant workers' problems? Has their situation improved? Or is there still work to do?

Do some research. The National Center for Farmworker Health provides lots of information about the conditions under which migrant farmworkers labor. Check out the group's website, www.ncfh.org, and then search the internet for other articles about migrant farmworkers. Are they better off than they were sixty years ago?

DIVE IN!

Cesar Chavez: A Photographic Essay by Ilan Stavans (Cinco Puntos Press, 2010), 91 pages.

Dolores Huerta Stands Strong: The Woman Who Demanded Justice by Marlene Targ Brill (Ohio University Press, 2018), 92 pages.

Did you know that thousands of children and teens work as farm laborers in the US? Many of them travel from place to place, following the harvest and changing schools several times a year. If young farmworkers go to your school, what can you do to make them feel welcome?

Chavez's nonviolent demonstrations eventually resulted in tens of thousands of agricultural workers enjoying higher pay, family health coverage, pension benefits, and other protections that came from working under United Farm Workers contracts.

ROBERTO CLEMENTE

"AN MVP ON AND OFF THE FIELD"
ATHLETE
HUMANITARIAN

Four-time batting champion
National League Most Valuable Player (MVP)—
  1966
Twelve-time winner of the Gold Glove Award
  for fielding proficiency
MVP, World Series—1971
Eleventh player to achieve 3,000 hits in a
  major-league career

As a member of the Pittsburgh Pirates baseball team, Roberto Clemente racked up a list of super statistics. But if that's all you know about him, you don't really know what makes Roberto Clemente a hero. It's more than MVP honors. It's the quality of his life and his giving.

Raised in a loving family, he learned important values as a child that would guide him for the rest of his life. Work hard. Do the very best you can. Be humble. Always care about others.

And Clemente did care about others. For many years, even after becoming one of baseball's great players, he would spend the off-season helping others with his time and energy as well as his money. When a terrible earthquake destroyed much of the city of Managua in the Central American country of Nicaragua, he wanted to help. He organized relief efforts to take food and medical supplies

In 1973 Roberto Clemente was inducted into the National Baseball Hall of Fame in Cooperstown, New York.

there. When he heard that supplies were being stolen and weren't reaching those who needed them, he was outraged. He decided to deliver the provisions personally, insisting, "They will not dare to steal from Roberto Clemente."

On New Year's Eve in 1972, he boarded a rickety old DC–7 cargo plane and took off on his mission. Moments after takeoff, the plane went down, killing everyone on board. Clemente's body was never found.

"Any time you have the opportunity to accomplish something for somebody who comes behind you and you don't do it, you are wasting your time on this earth."

—*Roberto Clemente*

Days later, the Baseball Writers of America elected Roberto Clemente to the Hall of Fame, waiving the requirement that a player must be retired for five years. What a tribute to his achievements on and off the playing field.

EXPLORE!

Only a few people can become MVPs in the sports world, but every one of us can be an MVP in life by helping other people as Roberto Clemente did. Read his Power Words. He's telling us to make things better in our world.

We're not necessarily talking about finding a cure for cancer or filling a plane with supplies for the poor. We're talking about the little things you can do every day—at school, at home, with your friends, whatever. For example, when was the last time you did an extra chore at home without being asked? Without complaining? Check your conscience. Look around you at school. Any way to make things better there?

What you do to "make things better" is up to you. You might collect food for a food bank . . . teach your little brother how to tie his shoes . . . empty the dishwasher . . . send a card to your grandmother . . . you figure it out!

Need a little inspiration? Read the Dive In! biography, or visit the official Clemente Museum website at www.clementemuseum.com. Find out about Roberto's Kids at www.robertos-kids.org. The group uses baseball to help develop strong communities. For even more inspiration, visit www.robertoclementefoundation.com. Make the time. Make the commitment. Make it happen.

Clemente posed for this photo in the 1950s. He played eighteen seasons for the Pittsburgh Pirates.

DIVE IN!

10 at 10: The Surprising Childhoods of Ten Remarkable People by Carlyn Beccia (Carolrhoda Books, 2021), 56 pages.

WALT DISNEY

DECEMBER 5, 1901–DECEMBER 15, 1966

THE FIRST IMAGINEER
ANIMATOR
FILMMAKER
DREAMER

This photo of Walt Disney was taken in 1950. One of his most famous creations appears in the background: Mickey Mouse.

Disney is possibly the most recognized name in the world! But how much do you know about the real man named Disney . . . Mickey's dad . . . the man who taught us to "Wish upon a Star"?

Hardly anyone believed it would work. "The idea is flawed." "People won't pay attention." "It's a waste of time, money, and talent." Not exactly words of encouragement. But Walt Disney believed in the project, and since he was the company's founder and driving force, it was going to happen. His brother, Roy, had learned long before not to try to talk Walt out of something he wanted to do.

It took about three years (1934–1937) to finish it, and it cost almost $1.5 million, an enormous amount of money in the midst of the country's Great Depression (1929–1939). But on December 21, 1937, all the doubters and disbelievers had to admit that they were wrong. The project that competitors had labeled "Disney's Folly" was an overnight smash hit, and it changed the world of entertainment forever. What are we talking about? Maybe you've seen it—a little masterpiece called *Snow White and the Seven Dwarfs*, the very first full-length animated movie ever made.

Today, we can watch full-length feature cartoons with excellent artwork, computer animation, memorable music, and big-name stars supplying voices for the princesses and talking animals on the screen. But Walt Disney began this phenomenon with a sketchbook and a dream. His imagination evolved into a new kind of worldwide entertainment.

Walt once said, "It's kind of fun to do the impossible."

DIVE IN!
Walt Disney: Drawn from Imagination by Bill Scollon (Disney Press, 2014), 132 pages.

EXPLORE!
Bet you thought we were going to send you off to Walt Disney World or Disneyland for this one. No such luck!

It's time you know more about the original "imagineer"—the clever name given to the creative people at the Disney studios. They are imaginative engineers.

Read the biography we suggest in Dive In! and get to know the man who made the magic happen. How did he handle failure? What inspired him? What made him laugh? Then visit the Walt Disney Family Museum at www.waltdisney.org. You'll find so many ways to use your imagination. Take an online class. Make a flip-book. Try a coloring project. Explore the website and use what you learn to design a new attraction for the Disney theme parks. Let your creativity soar!

Walt Disney loved to have fun. In this photo taken in his office on December 23, 1965, he pretends to read a movie script to a dog. You can see photos like this and much more at the Walt Disney Family Museum in San Francisco, California.

POWER WORDS!

"Somehow, I can't believe there are many heights that can't be scaled by a man who knows the secret of making dreams come true." —*Walt Disney*

DOROTHEA DIX

APRIL 4, 1802–JULY 17, 1887

VISIONARY AND ADVOCATE FOR THE MENTALLY ILL
POLITICAL ACTIVIST
AUTHOR AND EDUCATOR
HUMANITARIAN

Can an individual really make a difference? What if that person is a woman at a time when men dominated politics in the United States? Dorothea Dix proved it was indeed possible. She used evidence of mistreatment to help people with mental illnesses. And she placed herself in difficult and unpleasant surroundings to gather that evidence.

Her concern for others came from her difficult childhood and her strong Unitarian religious convictions. When she was just twelve years old, Dix left home to live with her grandmother to escape an alcoholic and abusive father and a mother struggling with mental illness. As a young woman, Dix spent time in England with Quakers who were trying to improve treatment of people with mental illness, and this also shaped her thinking.

The defining moment in Dix's life came when she began teaching a Sunday school class for women in a prison in her home state of Massachusetts. As she spoke with the inmates, she learned that a number of them had never been convicted of a crime. They were in prison because of mental illness. Dix decided she had to find a way to change how her state treated people with mental health problems.

Visiting jails and poorhouses all around Massachusetts, Dix saw firsthand what was happening to people in those places. She saw

This oil painting of Dorothea Dix hangs in the Smithsonian National Portrait Gallery in Washington, DC.

them put in cages and pens, as if they were animals. She saw them stripped naked, and she watched in horror as they were beaten with whips and rods so they would obey the guards' orders.

Conditions for mentally ill people in Massachusetts had to change. Dix set out to transform the system and make hospitals safer places. In a report to the state legislature, she detailed how people were treated like prisoners instead of like patients. After her report, the state expanded and improved a hospital in Worcester to help mentally ill people. Dix had been successful in her state, but she did not stop there.

Dix decided to devote her energies to reforming the care of people in other states as well. Over the course of just three years, she traveled more than 30,000 miles (48,300 km), an amazing feat in the 1840s! In state after state, she documented the disgusting conditions endured by mentally ill people. Using her eyewitness accounts as evidence, Dix persuaded men in power in states such as New York and North Carolina to establish humane asylums, or hospitals.

One determined woman—armed with conviction and evidence—convinced the men who held power that they too must show compassion to others.

POWER WORDS!

"In a world where there is so much to be done, I felt strongly impressed that there must be something for me to do." —*Dorothea Dix*

DIVE IN!

Dorothea Dix: Advocate for Mental Health Care by Margaret Muckenhoupt (Oxford University Press, 2003), 127 pages.

EXPLORE!

Guess what? There is something for YOU to do too—like Dorothea Dix's Power Words suggest for herself. What is YOUR something? If you don't know, there are lots of ideas from the 60 heroes in this book. As you read about the things that inspire them, think about something that inspires you. YOUR something should be meaningful for others as well as for yourself.

Maybe you already know what your something is. Hooray for you! Share it with others on social media. Share it with people at school, at your place of worship, and with your friends. YOUR something should be something you feel so good about that you want to share it.

Having a hard time deciding what YOUR something could be? Search online for the causes that inspire the heroes in this book. Read the books we suggest in the Dive In! sidebar for each hero. Talk to your family and friends about what excites them and makes them want to go the extra mile. Ask them why they care.

Can you and a friend share something that inspires you to act? Of course—that's called teamwork! Finding YOUR something and then working to achieve it will make you a hero too. Hero number 61!

EXPLORE SOME MORE!

Did you know that Dorothea Dix was the superintendant of army nurses for the Union army during the Civil War? She was a strong leader. Do you have a strong leader in your life? Write that person a note to say thank you.

This is the exterior of the Dorothea Dix Hospital in Raleigh, North Carolina. The hospital treated patients for more than 150 years.

FREDERICK DOUGLASS

THE VOICE OF FREEDOM
ABOLITIONIST
AUTHOR
ORATOR

Right now, you're doing what for Frederick Douglass was an illegal activity that enabled him to become a freeman. You are reading.

It was against the law to teach an enslaved person to read and write. If an enslaved person could read, that person might start to think about ideas such as freedom, justice, and fairness. That sounded like trouble to enslavers. But Mrs. Auld didn't know the law when eight-year-old Frederick was given to her family.

Frederick had lots of chores to do in the house, but life at the Auld home in Baltimore was better than he'd ever known—his enslaver actually taught him to read.

Then Mrs. Auld told her husband of Frederick's rapid progress and his eagerness to read. Mr. Auld had a fit! He knew the law. He knew how important it was to keep enslaved people from learning to read. He ordered her to stop.

But it was too late. The seeds of Frederick's freedom had been sown. He found other ways to continue to learn. White playmates helped him when they could. The enslavers were right. Reading did teach Frederick about freedom, justice, and fairness. And he wanted some, for himself and for every other enslaved person in the land.

Frederick Douglass's life spanned nearly eighty years, from the time that slavery was common in the United States to the time it was becoming a memory—a change in which he played a major role.

When he was twenty years old, Douglass escaped from slavery. As a freeman, he enthusiastically joined the abolitionists—the antislavery activists who were working hard to end the nightmare. He gave powerful speeches describing and denouncing the horrors of slavery. He established an antislavery newspaper called *North Star* and directed a branch of the Underground Railroad, which was the route north for freedom seekers.

At one point, Douglass's opponents tried to use his skills as a writer and orator to discredit

"No man can put a chain about the ankle of his fellow man without at last finding the other end fastened about his own neck." —*Frederick Douglass*

him. They insisted that he was too impressive to have been enslaved. That's when he wrote his famous autobiography, the *Narrative of the Life of Frederick Douglass: An American Slave*.

Slavery had stolen Frederick Douglass's childhood, destroyed his family, and abused generations of his people. He vowed to see it struck down. And indeed he did. The American Civil War was fought, Lincoln issued his Emancipation Proclamation, Congress enacted the Thirteenth Amendment to the Constitution, and slavery was gone. Thanks, in part, to an eight-year-old enslaved child who learned to read.

EXPLORE!

Frederick Douglass was very young when his enslaver's wife turned him on to the power of

DIVE IN!

Abraham Lincoln and Frederick Douglass: The Story behind an American Friendship by Russell Freedman (Houghton Mifflin Harcourt, 2012), 128 pages.

Facing Frederick: The Life of Frederick Douglass, a Monumental American Man by Tonya Bolden (Abrams, 2020), 200 pages.

the written word. Learning to read changed his life and eventually moved him to try to change the lives of people wrapped in slavery's chains.

So why don't *you* change someone's life? *You* can read, but not everyone can. Many students struggle with reading every day. Their parents or teachers often don't have time to give them the extra help they need. But *you* have time. Ask your teacher or guidance counselor if there's a tutoring program you can help with. Call your local library to see if they need someone to read to the little kids or help older ones with research projects.

ProLiteracy is a nonprofit organization dedicated to helping adults learn to read. Check out their website: www.proliteracy.org. Is there a local chapter in your community? Get in touch with the United Way (www.unitedway.org) headquarters in your area. They usually have a directory of service groups. Maybe you can join one that helps people learn to read.

Who knows? The person you read with today could become an American hero every kid should meet. Wouldn't it be cool to know that *you* helped make it happen?

Renowned for his eloquence, Douglass lectured throughout the United States and Great Britain on the brutalities of slavery. Here, Douglass (*right*) meets with Abraham Lincoln (*left*) during the Civil War.

MARIAN WRIGHT EDELMAN

JUNE 6, 1939–

FOUNDER OF THE CHILDREN'S DEFENSE FUND
LAWYER
ACTIVIST
AUTHOR

The Children's Defense Fund (CDF) has a simple goal: "to make sure every child in America has what they need to thrive." But what do children need to thrive, and how can adults give it to them?

Ask Marian Wright Edelman these questions, and she will be happy to explain. She has spent her life writing and speaking about why *all* children need to have equal opportunities. That means access to good schools, nutrition, and health care.

When Edelman graduated from Yale Law School in 1963, she didn't see that happening for kids. Far too often in the United States, children of color and children from poor families suffer. So Edelman took action. In 1973 she founded the CDF. The group has helped pass many laws that help children have better lives, including the 1974 Child Abuse Prevention and Treatment Act and the 1990 Americans with Disabilities Act. Edelman was the group's president until her retirement in 2018 when she became president emerita. As president emerita, she stepped away from her daily duties with the CDF but kept her title as an honor.

Marian Wright Edelman stands in front of a CDF banner in 1987. The CDF believes that fixing social problems in the United States begins with helping children.

How did Marian Wright Edelman become so passionate about her cause? She was partly inspired by her father, Arthur Wright, a Baptist minister in a small town in the segregated South. He believed being a good Christian required service to others. When Black kids were forbidden to play in the town's playgrounds, Marian, her father, and her four siblings went into action. They built a playground behind her father's church for all kids to use.

"If you don't like the way the world is, you change it. You have an obligation to change it. You just do it, one step at a time." —*Marian Wright Edelman*

DIVE IN!

Taking Action to Improve People's Health by Eric Braun (Lerner Publications, 2017), 48 pages.

Her father's lessons of inclusion have stayed with Edelman her entire life. So too have her father's final words to her before he died: "Don't let anything get in the way of your education." Edelman had the strength and desire to excel in high school, college, and law school. She knows the power that comes with an education.

Marian Wright Edelman (*back row, third from right*) poses with parents and children who received health care from a mobile clinic in Mississippi. Wright and the CDF know that children need good health care to thrive.

EXPLORE!

We have a tough question for you. Ready? What do you think *you* can do to help kids thrive in your school and community?

Before you answer, talk to your friends about this question. Tell them about Marian Wright Edelman and the CDF. Share and explore the group's website with them: www.childrensdefense.org.

The CDF is dedicated to meeting kids' basic needs such as food, school supplies, and education. How can *you* help provide those things in your community? Here are some ideas:

- Volunteer for groups in your area that provide food to people who need it.
- Find out if your community collects school supplies for kids who need new backpacks, pencils, and notebooks. How can you help?

- Volunteer for a summer program at a library, community center, or assisted-living facility. Help with crafts, reading, and cooking activities. What skills are you good at? What abilities can you share? Many people just want to hang out with someone who cares.

The point is simple—*you* can make a difference in the life of another kid.

EXPLORE SOME MORE!

Some activities run by the CDF invite kids like you to participate. Check out CDF Freedom Schools at https://www.childrensdefense.org /programs/cdf-freedom-schools/about-the -program/, and ask a grown-up how you can get involved!

THOMAS ALVA EDISON

THE WIZARD OF MENLO PARK
INVENTOR
GENIUS

A US patent is a special piece of paper issued by the government. All you have to do is invent something no one else has, and then you own that invention. The patent paper is proof that you did it. Thomas Alva Edison took out 1,093 patents during his eighty-four years on the planet. If he had invented one new thing each day, that translates into three solid years' worth of one-of-a-kind ideas.

During his lifetime, Edison was the most famous American in the world. His inventions include the incandescent light (you call it a light bulb), the phonograph (great-granddaddy of your digital music player), and the motion picture (as in "movie") projector. So much of what we use and enjoy today was born in Thomas Edison's creative mind. He was a genius.

When Tom was a boy, his teachers thought he was stupid because he asked so many questions. But his mom understood his never-ending need to know.

Tom was a genius, but he was also a master of trial and error. If something did not work, Edison always kept trying! He never seemed to get discouraged. He always believed that eventually he would succeed.

For a complete list of Edison's 1,093 successful US patent applications, go to http://edison.rutgers.edu/patents.htm. As you look at the list, keep in mind that Edison also filed as many as 600 unsuccessful patent applications.

POWER WORDS!

"Genius is one percent inspiration and ninety-nine percent perspiration."

—*Thomas Alva Edison*

When he set out to invent a storage battery, he probably didn't expect it to take 8,001 attempts to find a material that would hold an electrical charge. But when asked about this invention, he replied, "Well, at least we know 8,000 things that *don't* work." Edison proved that success comes to those who never quit.

EXPLORE!

Visit these Edison museums online to learn more about the inventor:

Edison and Ford Winter Estates
https://www.edisonfordwinterestates.org

The Thomas Edison Birthplace Museum
https://tomedison.org/

Thomas Edison National Historical Park
https://www.nps.gov/edis

Now conduct 9,990 experiments. Why? Well, that's how many tries it took Edison before he successfully found the right filament (wire) to make a light bulb glow. What if he had quit after 9 tries? After 90? After 900? How about 9,000? But he didn't give up. Edison wanted to be successful, and he was willing to put the time and effort into getting there. Actually, he probably *enjoyed* the process of trying out his ideas.

We want you to think about the stuff *you* do. Make a list: school projects, music lessons, sports practices.

Examine your attitude! Ask a few questions:

- Do you start on a project believing that you can succeed?

A photo of Thomas Edison from around 1925

- Do you see mistakes as lessons learned or time wasted?
- Is your motto "If at first you don't succeed, try, try again?"
- Are you willing to try? Are you willing to fail?
- Are you willing to try again?

Now decide you're going to do something better. Put Thomas Edison's picture where you'll see it a lot, such as on the refrigerator or your computer screen or your mirror. When you want to give up, stare at his face. Let him inspire you.

EXPLORE SOME MORE!

Can you be an inventor? Yes you can! Visit https://wisconsin.pbslearningmedia.org /collection/dsgclubs/ to learn about invention activities, how your inventions can help people, and ways to start your own inventions club.

DIVE IN!

Inventing the Future: A Photobiography of Thomas Alva Edison by Marfé Ferguson Delano (National Geographic, 2015), 64 pages.

ALBERT EINSTEIN

MARCH 14, 1879–APRIL 18, 1955

SCIENCE SUPERSTAR
GENIUS
PHYSICIST (SCIENTIST)

E$=mc^2$. It's probably the most well-known equation in all of science. "Energy equals mass times the speed of light times the speed of light." It may sound like a nonsense phrase to you, but E=mc^2 unlocked the secret of the atom and led the world into the nuclear age.

It is one of the great contradictions of modern times. Albert Einstein, a man known as a firm supporter of world peace, convinced President Franklin D. Roosevelt to launch a program to build an atomic bomb. The year was 1939, a fateful year for world peace. Hitler's Nazi troops were on the move. Einstein had fled Germany, the country of his birth, years earlier because of its horrible policies against Jews. He had come to the United States to live in peace.

Einstein knew scientists in his old country had the intelligence to develop atomic weapons, and he knew that Hitler would force them to do so. Should the United States also build a weapon of mass destruction? Other scientists and US leaders persuaded Einstein to urge President Roosevelt to act. And so, after many sleepless nights, Einstein wrote a letter. The United States had to build a bomb. Roosevelt agreed. Several days later, Einstein wrote a second letter to the president. He said that when the bomb was developed, it should never be used against people. A demonstration of its awesome power would convince any enemy to surrender.

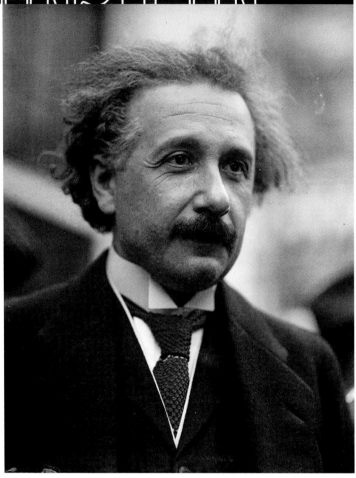

Albert Einstein's theories are still being studied. For example, he predicted the existence of gravitational waves about one hundred years ago, but it wasn't until 2016 that scientists had the technology to prove him right.

POWER WORDS!

"I don't know how the Third World War will be fought, but I do know how the Fourth will: with sticks and stones."

—*Albert Einstein*

So August 6, 1945, was a sad day for Albert Einstein. The first atomic bomb was dropped on the city of Hiroshima, Japan. The man of peace saw what he had feared so much come true.

EXPLORE!

You live in a world that can still blow itself up with nuclear weapons. Yes, the terrible Cold War (1945–1991) between the United States and the former Soviet Union (a union of republics that included Russia) is over. Both sides have destroyed some of their bombs, but far too many still exist.

Read Einstein's Power Words carefully. Do you see his meaning? These bombs can still destroy all of us if humans should ever be foolish enough to use them. Einstein knew that if such a thing happened, human society would be taken back to the Stone Age!

You should get busy and learn more about world peace. Why? Because as a future voter, you have to understand what is needed to keep our country and our world safe. Do you think our leaders should work to destroy all nuclear weapons? Or do we need to keep some "just in case"?

We hear you. "Hey, I'm just a kid! I'm worried about homework, my clothes, my future." Well, if we don't work to preserve world peace, you may not have a future. Get the picture? Visit www.kidsforpeaceglobal.org, a website packed with strategies for creating peace through friendship, kindness, and service.

DIVE IN!

Albert Einstein by Anita Croy (Crabtree, 2021), 64 pages.

Although Einstein's brilliant and original concepts ushered in the atomic age, he was an active pacifist who warned against the shocking destructive power of atomic bombs. The image at right shows a column of smoke rising from Nagasaki, Japan, after the United States dropped an atomic bomb on the city, August 9, 1945, near the end of World War II (1939–1945).

DWIGHT D. EISENHOWER

"I LIKE IKE"

GENERAL
US PRESIDENT
AUTHOR

What was it like to be in charge of one of the largest military invasions in the history of the world? Sounds like a plot for a movie, doesn't it? But US general Dwight D. "Ike" Eisenhower *lived* it as supreme commander of the Allied forces in World War II.

It's difficult for anyone who did not live through that terrible war to imagine how awful it was. Everything in an American's daily life was affected by the struggle to defeat the Axis powers of Germany, Japan, and Italy. World War II was massive, involving more than thirty countries and lasting for six years.

By 1944 Nazi Germany and their Italian partners controlled much of Europe. They had to be pushed back, and it was up to General Eisenhower to lead the way. His Great Crusade, as he called it, would attempt to free Europe from Nazi control. And it would begin on June 6, 1944—D-day.

Eisenhower and other Allied leaders kept the planning for D-day cloaked in total secrecy. Every detail of the landing on the beaches of Normandy, France, was rehearsed without the enemy discovering where and when the invasion would occur. From Normandy, Allied forces would spread out across Europe to battle Axis armies. Code-named Operation Overlord, the

Eisenhower is known as a great military leader, but he hated fighting. "War is a grim, cruel business, a business justified only as a means of sustaining the forces of good against the forces of evil," he said.

magnitude of the invasion was mind boggling in terms of the numbers of troops, ships, bombers, landing craft, guns and ammunition, medical supplies, and much more that converged on Normandy that day. And it fell upon one person's shoulders to make sure the invasion was a success. That individual was Ike.

Somehow, Eisenhower and the Allies pulled it off. June 6, 1944, will be a day forever celebrated for the Allied landing at Normandy and the beginning of the end of World War II in Europe. It was the largest seaborne invasion in history.

The invasion had originally been scheduled for June 5, but the supreme commander

"You are about to embark upon the Great Crusade, toward which we have striven these many months. The eyes of the world are upon you. The hopes and prayers of liberty-loving people everywhere march with you."

—Dwight D. Eisenhower

postponed it one day because of stormy weather. Even that decision was Ike's, and as usual, he made the right call.

EXPLORE!

On September 17, 2020, the Dwight D. Eisenhower Memorial was dedicated in Washington, DC. The memorial includes a life-size statue of Ike as a teenager. Kids who visit the Eisenhower memorial can look at that statue and think, "I can be like Ike!" As you learn more about this amazing hero, think about his lifetime of service to his country.

DIVE IN!

D-Day: The Invasion of Normandy, 1944 by Rick Atkinson (Henry Holt, 2014), 202 pages.

Dwight D. Eisenhower by Sarah Hansen (Child's World, 2020), 48 pages.

Commanding the Allied forces during D-day was one of many contributions Eisenhower made to the United States. He also served two terms as the nation's president during the Cold War (1945–1991) with the Soviet Union. It was a very dangerous period for the country.

Ike made many decisions as president that still affect the nation. The interstate highway system, which you may have been on many times, was created largely because of Eisenhower's strong support. Look for signs next time you are traveling on an interstate that proclaim "Eisenhower Interstate System." They show five stars in a circle above his name. Why do you think the signs have five stars?

EXPLORE SOME MORE!

Have you heard the slogan "I Like Ike"? It just might be the most famous three-word political slogan in American history! You can visit the website for the Dwight D. Eisenhower Presidential Library, Museum and Boyhood Home at www.eisenhower.archives.gov to discover all kinds of fascinating details about the thirty-fourth president.

Dwight D. Eisenhower posed for this photo in 1959 when he was president of the United States.

ANTHONY FAUCI

DECEMBER 24, 1940–

CHIEF MEDICAL ADVISER TO THE PRESIDENT
DIRECTOR OF THE NATIONAL INSTITUTE OF ALLERGY AND INFECTIOUS DISEASES
PHYSICIAN
SCIENTIST

Despite being a well-known medical doctor serving under seven US presidents, it wasn't until 2020 that nearly every American knew Anthony Fauci's name. The reason is simple—he became the face of the US response to the COVID-19 pandemic.

Since 1984 Fauci has been the director of the National Institute of Allergy and Infectious Diseases. He has served under seven different US presidents, including Ronald Reagan (see page 96), Barack Obama (see page 82), and Joe Biden.

Infectious diseases can be transmitted from one person to another. They include the flu, Ebola, and COVID-19. Fauci and the institute seek ways to prevent the spread of those diseases and to treat patients who get sick.

When COVID-19 began spreading in America in 2020, the country faced the largest health crisis since the 1918 flu pandemic. Fauci became a voice of reason to many Americans. In his television and social media broadcasts, he focused on the scientific facts related to COVID-19. He spoke in a calm manner and helped reassure the nation that we could get through this crisis if we worked together.

Fauci encouraged people to wear masks that covered the nose and mouth in public,

Anthony Fauci has written, cowritten, and edited more than fourteen hundred scientific publications.

and to avoid large social gatherings to prevent spreading COVID-19. He followed his own advice and was a role model for millions of Americans. When he turned eighty years old on Christmas Eve in 2020, he didn't have a big party, and his three daughters didn't travel to celebrate with him. Instead, Fauci celebrated at home with his wife. She arranged a video call with fifteen friends from around the world to surprise him with a birthday greeting.

One of Fauci's most important actions as a role model was to receive the COVID-19 vaccination live on national television. He was one of the first health-care workers to

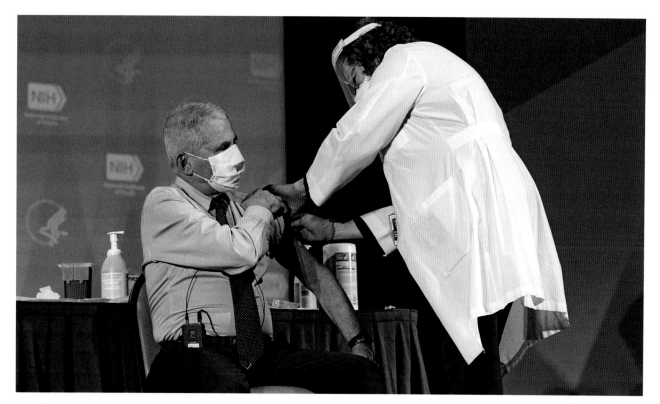

Fauci receives his first dose of a COVID-19 vaccine in December 2020. Being vaccinated helped Fauci protect his family, coworkers, and hospital patients from the disease.

receive the vaccine, and he expressed complete confidence that it was both safe and effective. What a strong demonstration by the leading fighter in our battle against COVID-19.

Some people don't believe what Fauci says about avoiding large crowds and wearing masks in public places. They speak out against him and sometimes say hateful things about him. But you know what? Americans are free to disagree with one another. Just remember to do your research and base your opinions on real facts!

EXPLORE!

You lived through the COVID-19 pandemic. Five years from now, what will you remember about this historic event? How about in ten years?

Think about the pandemic and how it affected you. Write your thoughts on paper, type them on a computer, or just say them out loud. Ask yourself questions to get started.

POWER WORDS!

"Wear a mask." —*Anthony Fauci*

Did you attend school in person, online, or both? Did you get used to wearing a mask over your nose and mouth? Did any of your family members get sick? Did you miss seeing some of your friends in person? How did you feel during the pandemic? Were you scared? Bored? Angry? Confused? Did you come up with creative ways to stay happy during this strange time?

Describe everything in detail so that in the future, when you read and remember your words, they will help your memories be clear.

Let's hope the world never faces another pandemic. But if it does happen again, maybe your own words from the past will give you some ideas about how to deal with it.

DIVE IN!

The COVID-19 Pandemic: A Coronavirus Timeline by Matt Doeden (Lerner Publications, 2021), 48 pages.

BENJAMIN FRANKLIN

JANUARY 17, 1706–APRIL 17, 1790

A MAN FOR ALL AGES
STATESMAN
INVENTOR
AUTHOR
DIPLOMAT
SCIENTIST
MUSICIAN
PHILOSOPHER
PUBLIC SERVANT

Franklin had a particular interest in electricity, a science that was in its infancy in 1749 when he successfully constructed the world's first electric battery. Franklin's most famous experiment involved flying a kite during a thunderstorm to prove that lightning is electricity.

Fish and visitors stink after three days."

Benjamin Franklin was a mastermind at creating one-liners. Franklin enjoyed having fun, and humor was a very important part of his life. His mind was always all over the place, dreaming up new ideas, new inventions, as well as new things to say.

He published many of his words of wisdom in *Poor Richard's Almanac*, which became one of the most popular books in the American colonies. Here's a sampling of Franklin's wise and witty sayings:

- "Be slow in choosing a Friend and slower in changing."
- "'Tis easier to prevent bad Habits than to break them."
- "Glass, China and Reputation are easily crack'd and never well mended."

The book made Dr. Franklin a wealthy man. And it gave him the money and the time to devote to his many other interests.

You probably know about some of the other things he did. Several of them were American "firsts." He founded the first public library, the first postal system, the first volunteer fire company, the first hospital, the first college in Philadelphia (the University of Pennsylvania), and he turned the citizens' "Night Watch" into the first Philadelphia police department. Add to that list of accomplishments the "discovery" of electricity in lightning (you know, the kite thing), the invention of the Franklin stove, bifocals, and the lightning rod and many other practical devices.

"Where liberty dwells, there is my country."

—Benjamin Franklin

But we have saved the best for last. Benjamin Franklin is the only person to have signed four of the most important documents in our country's history. He helped write all four too. Without these four documents, we might not be the country we are today. Can you name all four? We'll reveal the answers later.

EXPLORE!

Though Benjamin Franklin was born in Boston, Massachusetts, his adopted city was Philadelphia, Pennsylvania. That's where you'll find the Franklin Institute, an exciting scientific discovery museum. Franklin would have a great time visiting it in person or exploring its website:

The Franklin Institute
https://www.fi.edu

A favorite display at the Franklin Institute is a giant human heart. It's so big you can walk through it, following the path that a blood cell traces through the chambers of your heart. In the rotunda of the institute is the Benjamin Franklin National Memorial, where you'll find a 20-foot-high (6 m) marble statue of the man himself. The Franklin Institute's website and literature will tell you more about this fascinating place.

Also look into Franklin Court in Philadelphia, where Franklin's house once stood. The house was knocked down in 1812, but today you'll find a "Ghost Structure" there, an oversize steel skeleton that marks that spot. Also at the site are the United States Postal Service Museum, the Franklin Print Shop, and the underground Franklin Museum filled with his inventions. Check it out at https://www.nps.gov/inde/learn/historyculture/places-franklincourt.htm.

What about those four important documents that Franklin signed? Well, you're probably familiar with the most important ones: the Declaration of Independence and the US Constitution. In between signing them, he helped negotiate and sign the Treaty of Alliance with France, which brought the French army and navy to our side in the Revolutionary War (1775–1783), and the Treaty of Paris, which formally ended that war and recognized the United States as an independent country.

Thanks, Dr. Franklin!

DIVE IN!

Becoming Ben Franklin: How a Candle-Maker's Son Helped Light the Flame of Liberty by Russell Freedman (Holiday House, 2013), 86 pages.

Benjamin Franklin (*center right*) and other members of the Second Continental Congress are shown here presenting the Declaration of Independence to Congress.

RUTH BADER GINSBURG

MARCH 15, 1933–SEPTEMBER 18, 2020

SUPREME COURT JUSTICE
LAWYER
AUTHOR
POP CULTURE ICON
THE NOTORIOUS RBG

This official US Supreme Court portrait of Ruth Bader Ginsburg was taken in 2016. She usually wore a lace collar as a decoration with her judicial robes.

For Ruth Bader Ginsburg (RBG), a career path to the US Supreme Court was paved with challenges. She was smart, hardworking, and capable, but she was a *woman*. When RBG was young, many people didn't think that women should become lawyers or judges. Instead, they should stay home to raise families. No women served on the Supreme Court until 1981 when Justice Sandra Day O'Connor (see page 84) became the first.

At Harvard Law School in the 1950s, RBG and eight other women were the only female students in a class of five hundred. The law school's dean scolded the nine women for taking places that could have gone to men. But RBG was not discouraged. She worked hard and became an editor of the *Harvard Law Review* journal, a huge honor for an aspiring lawyer.

In 1958 when RBG's husband accepted a job in New York City after his Harvard Law School graduation, she transferred from Harvard to Columbia University to complete her law degree. She finished number one in her class.

A top student like RBG should have been flooded with job offers, but she wasn't. Women lawyers were still rare, and no law firm would hire her. She needed the help of a Columbia professor to finally find a job as a lawyer.

Unfortunately, for this and all of her early jobs, she made far less money than the men working beside her were paid. Ginsburg's personal struggle to be treated equally led her to become a champion for women's rights. She believed that everyone, regardless of gender, should be treated equally under the law.

In 1993 President Bill Clinton nominated RBG to the US Supreme Court. When she was

"Fight for the things that you care about but do it in a way that will lead others to join you."

—*Ruth Bader Ginsburg*

confirmed in August, she became just the second woman ever on the country's highest court. During her twenty-seven years as a US Supreme Court justice, RBG became an inspiration for millions, especially young girls. Rarely do individual justices gain much popularity, but RBG was someone special.

EXPLORE!

Who is Lilly Ledbetter, and how is she connected with Ruth Bader Ginsburg? Here's a clue: they both wanted employers to pay women and men equally for the same work, an issue that personally affected RBG and millions of others. Visit https://www.aauw.org/resources/faces-of -aauw/qa-lilly-ledbetter/ to learn more about Ledbetter, and then google the Lilly Ledbetter Fair Pay Act of 2009.

DIVE IN!

Becoming RBG: Ruth Bader Ginsburg's Journey to Justice by Debbie Levy (Simon & Schuster Books for Young Readers, 2019), 208 pages.

Dissenter on the Bench: Ruth Bader Ginsburg's Life and Work by Victoria Ortiz (Clarion Books, 2019), 199 pages.

EXPLORE SOME MORE!

Even in her late eighties, RBG stayed mentally sharp and physically strong. She worked out with a personal trainer twice a week for eighteen years to stay in great physical shape. What a super example of fitness for life! Google "Ruth Bader Ginsburg workout" to find descriptions of her fitness routine, and try it yourself. Time to get moving!

Ginsburg received the LBJ Liberty and Justice for All Award at a ceremony in Washington, DC, in January 2020, about eight months before her death in September.

JOHN GLENN

JULY 18, 1921–DECEMBER 8, 2016

WORLD'S OLDEST SPACE VOYAGER

ASTRONAUT
US SENATOR
1962 HEADLINE: *GLENN ORBITS EARTH!*
1998 HEADLINE: *GLENN ORBITS EARTH—
 AGAIN!*
AUTHOR

John Glenn is shown here just before his historic flight aboard *Friendship 7* in 1962. Later that year, he was awarded the NASA Distinguished Service Medal by President John F. Kennedy.

On October 29, 1998, Senator John Glenn boarded the space shuttle *Discovery* as part of a crew of seven astronauts. As *Discovery* climbed skyward for the nine-day mission, a National Aeronautics and Space Administration (NASA) spokesperson said, "Liftoff for six American heroes and one American legend." And she was right. Because seventy-seven-year-old John Glenn, who became the oldest person in the world ever to travel in space, was legendary.

Back in the 1960s, when President John F. Kennedy committed our nation to sending a manned mission to the moon, Americans loved the idea of exploring the "new frontier." We also loved the idea of entering a space race with our then number one enemy, the former Soviet Union.

On February 20, 1962, we took a big step forward. Alan Shepard, one of the original seven astronauts, flew into space in a suborbital flight. That was great, but it was not the same as the Soviets circling the planet. We were still behind.

Then, in a space capsule called *Friendship 7* (in honor of the seven astronauts), John Glenn closed the gap. Millions of Americans were glued to their television sets as Colonel Glenn's 93-foot (28 m)

Atlas rocket blasted into space. Inside his tiny capsule, Glenn repeated the final numbers of the countdown: "four, three, two, one, zero, ignition." Liftoff. He was on his way into outer space.

For the next five hours, he circled Earth three times. And Americans worried. Remember, we had never witnessed anything like this before. What if something went wrong? The slightest mechanical failure could mean disaster. Everything had to work perfectly. And everything did. Orbit, reentry, splashdown into the ocean, and the United States' newest hero had returned safely. The race was on, and the United States was ready.

"What benefits are we gaining from the money spent? They are probably not even known to man today. But exploration and the pursuit of knowledge have always paid dividends in the long run—usually far greater than anything expected at the outset." —*John Glenn (1962)*

"Going back to space, I had defied the expectations for my age." —*John Glenn (1998)*

EXPLORE!

So much has changed in the space program since it began more than sixty years ago. As you explore its beginnings and look at it today, we want you to ask yourself a very important question: Should the United States spend more or less money on space exploration in the next twenty years than it has in the past twenty years?

In our democracy, "we, the people" have a voice in answering that question through our elected representatives. It's an important question for you because yours is the generation that will be paying for future space exploration. But you have to be well informed to make a sound decision. Start by examining some space memorabilia (stuff with historical meaning) and books so you can learn about our space program, past and present.

NASA Headquarters
https://www.nasa.gov

NASA at Home—For Kids and Families
https://www.nasa.gov/nasa-at-home-for
-kids-and-families

**Smithsonian National Air and
Space Museum**
https://www.airandspace.si.edu

Liftoff: A Photobiography of John Glenn by Don Mitchell (National Geographic, 2006), 64 pages.

Rocket Man: The Mercury Adventure of John Glenn by Ruth Ashby (Peachtree, 2019), 117 pages.

EXPLORE SOME MORE!

From the International Space Station to private spaceflight, this is an exciting time for space exploration in the United States. NASA is even planning a trip to Mars! Read all about it by visiting www.nasa.gov and clicking on the "Moon to Mars" tab.

**John Glenn gives a
political speech in 2004.**

51

AMANDA GORMAN

MARCH 7, 1998–

NATIONAL YOUTH POET LAUREATE
ACTIVIST
AUTHOR

The 2021 US presidential inauguration was unlike any other in our country's history. Just fourteen days earlier, an angry and violent crowd attacked the United States Capitol, the site of the swearing-in ceremony. The crowd tried to block the formal Electoral College victory of President-elect Joe Biden and Vice President-elect Kamala Harris (see page 54). All of this was happening while the US and the world were in the midst of the deadly COVID-19 pandemic.

On January 20, 2021, Inauguration Day, security in our nation's capital was heavy. Police officers and military troops were everywhere. Yet as the solemn transition of power proceeded, young Black poet Amanda Gorman seized the moment and became a hero to tens of millions of viewers.

At twenty-two, Gorman became the youngest poet ever to speak at a presidential inauguration. She read "The Hill We Climb," a poem she had written for the occasion. After the riots of January 6, she added to her poem to reflect on her feelings about that dark day. But the tone of the poem remained uplifting, and her delivery was flawless. She challenged the country to come together and unify.

Do you know what makes her stunning performance that day even more remarkable? All of her life, Gorman has struggled to pronounce certain sounds, like the letter *r*. But that didn't stop her from addressing the nation

In 2017 Amanda Gorman became the first National Youth Poet Laureate in the United States. The title honors young poets committed to "artistic excellence, civic engagement, and social justice."

on January 20. Who knows what future hills this amazingly talented poet will climb?

EXPLORE!
Every year, the Alliance for Young Artists and Writers presents the Scholastic Art and Writing Awards to talented teens from all over the United States. Students can apply for awards in twenty-eight categories of art and writing. Does your school participate? Find out who the winners are, where you can read and view their work, and how *you* can compete for one of these

"For there is always light, if only we're brave enough to see it. If only we're brave enough to be it." —*Amanda Gorman*

Gorman reads a poem at the 2021 US presidential inauguration. Almost thirty-four million people watched the ceremony on TV.

awards. Who knows? You could be the next Amanda Gorman! Visit https://www.artandwriting.org/ to learn more.

EXPLORE SOME MORE!

Like Amanda Gorman, millions of people have trouble pronouncing certain sounds. Or, like President Biden, they may stutter when the flow of their speech is interrupted. Other people may have different problems with speech. If you have a hard time speaking or pronouncing certain words and are bothered by it, talk to adults who care about you. By working with a speech-language pathologist, or speech therapist, you'll be able to find things to do that can help. If you'd like to help people who have speaking problems, google "speech language therapist" to learn more about following this career path yourself.

DIVE IN!

Amanda Gorman by Megan Borgert-Spaniol (Abdo, 2022), 32 pages.

The Hill We Climb: An Inaugural Poem for the Country by Amanda Gorman (Viking, 2021), 29 pages.

KAMALA HARRIS

OCTOBER 20, 1964–

HISTORIC FIRST VICE PRESIDENT OF THE UNITED STATES
US SENATOR
LAWYER
AUTHOR

After forty-eight different men held the office for the first 233 years of our country's history, a woman finally became the US vice president. And she is a woman of color, representing both Black and South Asian Americans.

Kamala Harris's career before reaching the vice presidency was filled with one success after another. She was the first woman elected as the district attorney of San Francisco, California. Then she became California's first woman, first Black, and first South Asian attorney general. She later won election to become one of California's United States senators.

Harris's mother, Shyamala Gopalan, died twelve years before Harris's inauguration to become vice president. Harris says her mother was most responsible for starting her on a path to success. Harris loves sharing the story of her mother's amazing journey.

In 1958 nineteen-year-old Gopalan left her home in India to pursue her dream in the United States. She wanted to study biochemistry, but that subject was not offered to girls at the school she attended in India. So Gopalan executed a secret plan. Without the knowledge of her parents, she applied to the University of California, Berkeley. Moving to the US to attend the school was the first step of many that would

The official portrait of Vice President Kamala Harris is displayed in government buildings and other locations around the United States.

change the course of American history.

Harris's mother taught her to stand up for her principles. Gopalan became very active in the US civil rights movement in the 1960s, and Berkeley was a hotbed of activism. Harris attended protests with her mom, sometimes riding in a stroller!

Gopalan was a strong woman who taught her daughter to connect with the world beyond herself and open her mind and heart to those who are struggling. Harris keeps these lessons close to her heart as she serves the US as vice president.

"I may be the first woman to hold this office. But I won't be the last." —*Kamala Harris*

EXPLORE!

What does the US vice president do? According to the Constitution, the vice president presides over the Senate and votes if there is a tie. If the president can't fulfill their duties for some reason, the vice president takes over the highest office in the country.

Is that all the vice president does? We don't think so! What other responsibilities has Joe Biden assigned to Harris? How does her background help her perform these tasks? You might have suggestions about what she should do. Share them with her! Contact her through the White House website at https://www.whitehouse.gov/contact/. We would like to hear your ideas too. Tell us at https://heroes4us.com/contact-american-heroes/.

EXPLORE SOME MORE!

Harris is married to attorney Douglas Emhoff. When she took office in 2021, Emhoff became the first male spouse of a US vice president. The spouses of presidents and vice presidents often take on important issues to help the country. One of the heroes in this book, Eleanor Roosevelt (see page 102), was an accomplished and influential partner to President Franklin Roosevelt (see page 104). So what issues are important to Emhoff? Is he using his role in any special ways? Search online to learn more about him.

DIVE IN!

Kamala Harris by Kelsey Jopp (Focus Readers, 2020), 48 pages.

Harris places her left hand on two bibles as she recites the oath of office of the vice president. One of the bibles belonged to a family friend, and the other was the property of Thurgood Marshall, the first Black member of the US Supreme Court.

JOHN HERRINGTON

SEPTEMBER 14, 1958–

FIRST NATIVE AMERICAN IN SPACE

ASTRONAUT
ENGINEER
US NAVAL AVIATOR
AUTHOR

If you had a chance to travel to space, what would you take with you? Astronaut John Herrington took eagle feathers, arrowheads, a hand-carved wooden flute, and flags of the Chickasaw and Crow peoples. These objects represent his heritage. Herrington, a member of the Chickasaw Nation, was the first Native American astronaut to reach space.

Working for NASA fulfilled one of Herrington's childhood dreams. When he was eight years old, he imagined flying to the moon in a rocket ship he had made out of a cardboard box. Years later, NASA chose him to train for a *real* spaceflight.

Preparing for a space mission is grueling. Herrington spent two years with fellow trainees enduring all kinds of physical and mental challenges. His experience as a US Navy pilot paid off and helped him meet the challenges and overcome them.

November 23, 2002, was Herrington's big day. He climbed aboard *Endeavour* and began his work as a mission specialist on the sixteenth space shuttle flight to the International Space Station (ISS). He was in space for thirteen days, eighteen hours, and forty-seven minutes. During that time, Herrington went on three space walks! For almost twenty hours, he worked *outside* of the ISS!

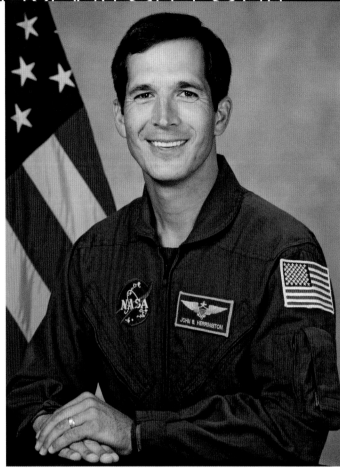

John Herrington posed for this picture in 1996, the year he officially became a NASA astronaut and began training to travel to space.

Back on Earth, Herrington travels around the United States. He speaks to groups about his role in America's exploration of space and his pride in being a member of the Chickasaw Nation.

EXPLORE!

The ISS is still orbiting our planet, and you can see it without a telescope. Visit https://spotthestation.nasa.gov/ to find out where and when to view the ISS in orbit. Astronauts from different nations are working on it every day, and some of them have stayed in space for long periods. What is the most time any astronaut

"Honor and respect people of all ethnicities; we're all on this team together and have the same goal." —*John Herrington*

has spent on the ISS? Search for the answer, and you will be amazed when you discover more about this person!

Since Herrington went to space, so much has changed about the US space program and how it operates. The biggest difference is how the astronauts travel to and from the ISS. NASA's space shuttle program is no longer active, so private companies like SpaceX and the Russian space program are responsible for that job. SpaceX is developing reusable rockets to make space travel more affordable.

Here's where your experience as an internet researcher comes into play. To begin, search for "private space companies." SpaceX might be the one you've heard about the most, but don't stop there. A number of other private companies compete with SpaceX.

DIVE IN!

Hidden Heroes in Space Exploration by Dionna L. Mann (Lerner Publications, 2023), 32 pages.

Next, explore the NASA website (www.nasa.gov) to learn about exciting goals for our country in space. You can even find out what it takes to become an astronaut. Interested in traveling to space? GO FOR IT!

EXPLORE SOME MORE!

The accomplishments of Native Americans in the space program, including John Herrington's space walks, are honored on a special 2019 US dollar coin. It is part of the US Mint's Native American $1 Coin Program. On the other side of the coin is Sacagawea (see page 72). What other Native American space pioneer appears on the coin? To find out, visit https://www.usmint.gov/coins/coin-medal-programs/native-american-dollar-coins/2019-american-indians-in-space.

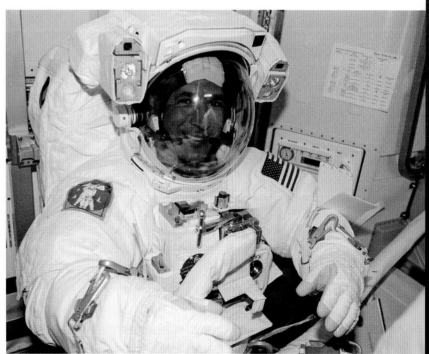

Herrington wears a space suit for his first space walk in November 2002. The space suit provides astronauts with oxygen, heat, and water, and protects them from the harsh conditions of space.

MILTON HERSHEY

THE CHOCOLATE KING
ENTREPRENEUR (BUSINESS RISK TAKER)
PHILANTHROPIST

Chocolatetown, USA: where Chocolate Avenue and Cocoa Avenue meet, where the street lamps are shaped like candy "Kisses," where chocolate is the biggest business in town. Sounds like a fantasy place in a kids' book, doesn't it? Well, don't tell that to the people in Hershey, Pennsylvania. It's their home!

Hershey chocolates are world famous—now. But in the beginning, the famous and wealthy Milton Hershey was a terrible failure in the candy business. First, he failed in Philadelphia. Next, he failed in Denver. Then he failed in Chicago, New Orleans, and New York City. Yes, Milton Hershey racked up failures in some of the greatest cities in the United States. So he returned to Lancaster, Pennsylvania, where he had spent part of his youth. A dear friend lent him some money, and Hershey—believe it or not—*again* tried the candy business. This time he made caramels. Even his mother and his aunt helped him.

Milton was selling his candy from a pushcart along the streets of Lancaster when a visiting Englishman tasted his caramels. That Englishman happened to be a candy importer, and he *loved* Milton's caramels. He wanted to send lots of them back to Great Britain. Suddenly, the Hershey caramel business was booming! Milton made a million dollars. Then he decided to launch a brand-new candy business (chocolates) in a brand-new town (Hershey!). And as they say, the rest is history.

Milton Hershey on November 23, 1923. If you visit the town of Hershey, be sure to stop at the Hershey Story museum (www.hersheystory.org).

EXPLORE!

Hershey, Pennsylvania, is not only home to the leading manufacturer of chocolate products in North America, to an amusement park and Chocolate World attraction, and to other delights, it's also home for Hershey's kids!

Milton and his wife Kitty were unable to have children of their own, so they decided to start a home for orphan boys. Today, the vast complex of homes and schools serves the educational and family needs of over twenty-one hundred children. It's a wonderful continuing memorial to the Hersheys and their desire to use their money to help others. The Hersheys were philanthropists. Maybe you've come across

"I often hear people say that 'children are not what they used to be.' But I have the conviction that they are just what they always have been. Perhaps it is the parents who have changed." —*Milton Hershey*

this word before. Philanthropists are people who use their money to help others less fortunate than they. The big philanthropists get lots of major credit, such as the Hersheys, the Gates, the Carnegies (built lots of libraries), the Fords, the Rockefellers. Check out philanthropy on the internet and see what you find.

But you too can be a philanthropist. Buy one less candy bar a week, and put that money in a special "Philanthropy Jar." By December holiday time, you'll have enough money in your jar to buy a toy or something else for a child in need. The money in your Philanthropy Jar will help you touch someone's life. It's a great start. Your place of worship or community charity groups can help you find a child who needs a present. Write a note to go along with your gift. Encourage that child, whom you've probably never met, to never give up, to keep trying, and to have hope.

That's what Milton and Kitty did. Over the years, their generous philanthropy has given hope to tens of thousands of children.

DIVE IN!

Chocolate by Hershey: A Story about Milton S. Hershey by Betty Burford (Millbrook Press, 1994), 64 pages.

Milton Hershey: Hershey's Chocolate Creator by Joanne Mattern (Abdo, 2015), 48 pages.

Although he had no children of his own, Milton Hershey generously contributed toward the well-being and education of thousands of children. To this day, the Milton Hershey School offers children education, housing, clothing, meals, medical and dental care, and recreational activities.

TEAM HOYT

FATHER AND SON SUPERATHLETES
RUNNERS
PIONEERS
HUMANITARIANS

Dick Hoyt *(left)* and his son Rick posed for this photo before a race in Holland, Massachusetts, on May 5, 2010.

YES YOU CAN!

When Rick Hoyt was fifteen years old, he wanted to take part in a 5-mile (8 km) benefit run to help a young person who had been in an accident. Rick shared his wish with his dad, who agreed to do everything he could to help Rick make it happen. For many teenagers a run like this wouldn't be such a big deal. But Rick was born with cerebral palsy. Cerebral palsy is a brain disorder that affects muscles and the way people move. Rick couldn't walk or speak. But that didn't stop Rick and his dad, Dick, from dreaming big. Dick would serve as his son's legs in the 5-mile run, pushing Rick to the finish line in a wheelchair.

Facing challenges head-on was nothing new to the Hoyts. Rick has cerebral palsy because his umbilical cord was wrapped around his neck during birth. The cord interfered with Rick's airflow and injured his brain.

Many people doubted that Rick would ever live a productive life. Doctors advised that Dick and his wife, Judy, put Rick into a long-term care facility. He would spend his life in a hospital. But his parents didn't listen to that advice.

Rick and Judy fought to make it possible for Rick to attend public school. They had a special computer made that allowed Rick to communicate, unlocking the smart boy inside.

POWER WORDS!
"Dad, when I'm running, it feels like I'm not handicapped." —*Rick Hoyt*

He went on to graduate from high school before attending Boston University. He graduated in 1993 with a degree in special education.

Their spirit of accomplishment and tenacity kept Rick and his dad going when they completed their first 5-mile run. At the time, they had no idea that they were beginning a long, inspiring journey. They became known as Team Hoyt, and YES YOU CAN! became their motto. Over the next few decades, Team Hoyt would compete in more than one thousand races, including marathons, duathlons, and triathlons. They even completed six Ironman competitions! Rick and his dad finished thirty-two Boston Marathons, one of America's most famous races. In 1992 they even tackled a trip all the way across the United States that covered 3,735 miles (6,011 km) in forty-five days!

Team Hoyt—born of love, determination, and a father's message to his son: YES YOU CAN!

EXPLORE!

Do you think Rick is the only person with a disability who has achieved amazing athletic feats? Not at all! Rick and Dick's story has inspired others with disabilities to say, "Yes I can!" Your challenge is to learn about other athletes like Team Hoyt and then share their stories with your friends and family.

Start by exploring the Team Hoyt website (www.teamhoyt.com), and read about others who have been inspired by Dick and Rick's feats. You can learn about some of the ways people with disabilities remain active, vital members of society.

In 2013 Team Hoyt was honored with a special ESPN award called the Jimmy V Award for Perseverance. Google it to learn more about other amazing people

DIVE IN!

Devoted: The Story of a Father's Love for His Son by Dick Hoyt with Don Yaeger (Da Capo, 2010), 203 pages.

who have received the award.

What about in your school and community? Are there individuals with disabilities who have reached athletic achievements that seemed impossible? What about outside of sports? Can you find people with disabilities in the performing arts, such as music, dance, and acting? Don't forget the visual arts such as painting and sculpting.

Use social media to share the awesome stories you discover. Maybe you can include them in a school writing project. And don't forget to let us know about these incredible individuals too. Go to www.heroes4us.com to share the stories you've uncovered. Author to authors! How cool is that?

EXPLORE SOME MORE!

You know about the Olympic Games, right? How about the Paralympic Games? This international sporting event involves exceptional athletes with special needs. Visit www.paralympic.org for more about this world of athletic competition.

In addition to marathons, Dick and Rick have competed in triathlons that include three stages: running, biking, and swimming.

LANGSTON HUGHES

FEBRUARY 1, 1902–MAY 22, 1967

HARLEM RENAISSANCE ICON
POET
AUTHOR
PLAYWRIGHT

Troubadour **is a word that usually refers to a poet-musician from medieval days.** But Americans had a troubadour during the Great Depression of the 1930s. He didn't sing, but did he ever read poetry—his own poetry.

You never know when someone else's words may change your life. That's what happened to young Langston Hughes. While he and a friend were on their way to Cuba for a vacation, they decided to stop in Daytona, Florida, to meet the famous Black educator Mary McLeod Bethune (see page 16). During their visit, she suggested that Hughes travel throughout the South reading his poetry to earn a living. The idea seemed kind of crazy to him. After all, this was the time of the Great Depression when almost everybody was having trouble finding work. Could he do this? "People need poetry," replied Bethune, "especially our people."

Weeks later, while driving back to New York, Langston Hughes made his decision. He would make poetry his career. A friend from his college days would serve as his driver and manager. They would travel through the South, holding poetry readings at colleges attended mostly by Black students. Langston Hughes wrote and read poetry that spoke of the experience of being Black, poetry that taught of the struggles of being Black in a segregated United States, poetry that gave a voice to a better life for Black Americans. And everywhere he spoke, the

Langston Hughes was one of the Harlem Renaissance troubadours who continued to be an artistic and commercial success after the nurturing environment of the movement ended.

audiences, mostly Black college students, greeted him eagerly. He reached them. His words stirred them, angered them, made them proud.

Langston Hughes joined other writers who led a Black cultural movement centered in New York. That movement was called the Harlem Renaissance, and Hughes became one of its most well-known troubadours. Like the troubadours of medieval days, he moved among his people, spreading a message.

EXPLORE!
How about writing some poetry?
Me? Poetry? No way! I wouldn't know what to write about.
Take a look at Langston Hughes's poetry. He wrote about who he was, his life experiences.

"Hold fast to dreams, for if dreams die, life is a broken-winged bird that cannot fly." —*Langston Hughes*

In addition to poetry, Langston Hughes wrote plays, prose, and even lyrics for musicals. He is shown here around 1945.

He wrote of being a Black person, of his travels, his emptiness. Learn from him and write about what you know. Write a poem about your life, a good friend, or a family member who is always there for you. Write about things that scare you or make you mad or give you hope. Sometimes Hughes wrote about problems. Give it a try. It's one way of helping yourself see a problem clearly and maybe finding a way to solve it.

Whether to share your poetry with others is a decision only you can make. Langston Hughes decided to share his, but some poets keep their work completely private or share it only with a close friend. Whatever you do with it, write it. Follow Langston Hughes's lead and allow your inner voice to speak.

DIVE IN!

Langston Hughes: Harlem Renaissance Writer by David H. Anthony and Stephanie Kuligowski (Teacher Created Materials, 2012), 32 pages.

Langston Hughes: Jazz Poet of the Harlem Renaissance by Charlotte Etinde-Crompton and Samuel Willard Crompton (Enslow, 2019), 104 pages.

THOMAS JEFFERSON

APRIL 13, 1743–JULY 4, 1826

AUTHOR OF THE DECLARATION OF INDEPENDENCE

US PRESIDENT
STATESMAN
AUTHOR
ARCHITECT
INVENTOR

On what day of the year did Thomas **Jefferson die?** Look at the top of the page. See it? Does that date ring a bell? A "Liberty Bell" maybe? Thomas Jefferson died on the Fourth of July, known as Independence Day since 1776. That year, our nation's founders adopted the Declaration of Independence, a document Jefferson had helped create, on July 4. Kind of ironic, isn't it? Jefferson's last day on the planet was the fiftieth birthday of the nation he helped create. And get this: Thomas Jefferson's good friend John Adams, the other man most responsible for that Declaration, died the very same day!

Thomas Jefferson was almost seventeen when he entered the College of William and Mary in colonial Virginia's capital, Williamsburg. Jefferson had always liked school. It wasn't unusual for him to spend fifteen hours a day studying, although he was definitely not an eighteenth-century bookworm. He loved horse racing, card playing, dancing, and playing the violin.

Teachers are powerful people. Good teachers can change your life, and that's what happened to young Thomas Jefferson in college. Dr.

In writing the Declaration of Independence, Jefferson carefully balanced the strength of government against the freedom and well-being of the individual.

William Small was a professor of mathematics and science. He gave Jefferson a love for learning how things work. For the rest of his life, Thomas Jefferson would try to understand *everything*: plants, animals, mechanical things, buildings. Dr. Small's influence eventually led his student to design a beautiful home called Monticello. Another teacher, lawyer George Wythe, became his law professor. Jefferson called him "my second father." Wythe taught the future author of our Declaration of Independence the principles of law found in that great document. And in 1776, teacher George Wythe became one of the fifty-six brave signers of his former student's greatest work, the Declaration of Independence.

EXPLORE!

Thomas Jefferson wrote his own epitaph. An epitaph is a statement that remembers and honors a person who has died and is often carved on a grave or a tomb. Of his many accomplishments, Jefferson wanted us to remember three specific things he did during his incredible life:

- authoring the Declaration of Independence
- authoring the Virginia Statute for Religious Freedom
- founding the University of Virginia

DIVE IN!

John Adams and Thomas Jefferson by Jill Keppeler (Gareth Stevens, 2022), 32 pages.

Thomas Jefferson's Presidency by Emily Rose Oachs (Lerner Publications, 2017), 104 pages.

Jefferson didn't include any of his important titles such as president, vice president, and secretary of state. He listed what he considered to be the greatest gifts he gave to the American people.

What do you hope your epitaph will say? We know you've probably thought about what you want to do when you're an adult—it's natural to think about your future. Maybe you've pictured the career you'll have or the places you'll live. What important things do you want to accomplish in life? Do you want to raise a family? Write poetry? Volunteer for a charity? Learn to paint? Maybe making a lot of money is important to you. How will you do it? You decide. Life's journey and its rewards can be measured in so many different ways.

EXPLORE SOME MORE!

You can see Jefferson's gravestone when you visit Monticello, the magnificent home he designed in Charlottesville, Virginia. To find out more about Monticello visit www.monticello.org.

POWER WORDS!

"All men are created equal, that they are endowed by their Creator with certain unalienable Rights, that among these are Life, Liberty and the pursuit of Happiness."

—*Thomas Jefferson (from the Declaration of Independence)*

KATHERINE JOHNSON

AUGUST 26, 1918–FEBRUARY 24, 2020

SPACE-AGE PIONEER
MATHEMATICIAN
GENIUS

If she says the numbers are good, I'm ready to go." Astronaut John Glenn (see page 50) said those words in 1962 before the launch of *Friendship 7*. Glenn rode the spaceship during the first US mission to orbit Earth.

"She" was Katherine Johnson, a Black mathematician and "human computer" who worked for NASA. The age of computers was still fairly new, and Glenn was uncomfortable knowing that the calculations for his flight had been made only by machines. He knew how brilliant Johnson was, and he insisted that she personally verify *by hand* all the computer-generated numbers that would dictate the mission's path, speed, and angle into space.

Johnson's life leading up to this moment was filled with accomplishments. A gifted student who loved math, she entered high school at the age of ten and started college at fifteen. Johnson graduated with honors and became a teacher. Then she heard that the National Advisory Committee for Aeronautics (later renamed NASA) was hiring Black women to solve math problems. *That* was the job she wanted! Johnson analyzed test-flight data and calculated flight paths, performing critical work on Alan Shepard's historic suborbital mission (see page 50). Johnson did the same work for Glenn and *Friendship 7*. She did the calculations

This official NASA portrait of Katherine Johnson was taken in 1971.

and guaranteed the accuracy of the computers, and the flight went forward successfully.

Johnson's work helped NASA land astronauts on the moon in 1969 and became essential for the development of NASA's space shuttle program. Even more extraordinary is that she performed her work despite facing two types of discrimination—race and gender. She endured hostile workplace conditions that may have led many other people to walk away from the jobs.

Johnson's desire to use her extraordinary mental gifts for her country enabled her to persevere. America and all of humankind benefited from her work as space exploration took off.

"If you approach any problem properly, you'll get the answer. If you don't get it the first time, you'll get it the second time." —*Katherine Johnson*

EXPLORE!

In 1963 Valentina Tereshkova of the Soviet Union became the first woman in space. Since then, many American women have joined the space program as astronauts, engineers, mathematicians, and more. Sally Ride, Mae Jemison, and Ellen Ochoa are just a few of the women to contribute to the US space program. Visit https://www.itu.int/en/myitu/News /2021/04/12/07/19/Women-in-space-history -International-Day-Human-Space-Flight to learn more about them and other talented women.

Their space careers were sparked by an interest in STEM—science, technology, engineering, and math. Visit https://www.nasa.gov/stem /womenstem.html to discover more women in STEM. Their stories will inspire you. Another notable female astronaut was Christa McAuliffe, a social studies teacher who trained to become the first civilian in space. Tragically, McAuliffe and six other astronauts died when the *Challenger* space shuttle exploded soon after takeoff. Learn more about McAuliffe and her "lost lessons" at https:// www.nasa.gov/feature/honoring-a-teacher-christa -mcauliffe-s-lost-lessons.

EXPLORE SOME MORE!

In 2016 the movie *Hidden Figures* helped people around the world realize how important Katherine Johnson and two of her Black coworkers, Dorothy Vaughan and Mary Jackson, were to the US space program. The film received many awards. Ask a grown-up if you can watch it. Maybe they will even watch it with you!

DIVE IN!

Reaching for the Moon: The Autobiography of NASA Mathematician Katherine Johnson by Katherine Johnson (Atheneum Books for Young Readers, 2019), 248 pages.

Barack Obama places the Presidential Medal of Freedom around Katherine Johnson's neck on November 24, 2015. The medal honors people who have made "especially meritorious contributions to the security or national interests of the United States, to world peace, or to cultural or other significant public or private endeavors."

HELEN KELLER AND ANNE SULLIVAN

KELLER: JUNE 27, 1880–JUNE 1, 1968

SULLIVAN:
APRIL 14, 1866–OCTOBER 20, 1936

THE MIRACLE WORKERS
AUTHOR
TEACHER
ACTIVISTS

Water. It's necessary for all life. You drink it, bathe in it, swim in it. It's always there. For Helen Keller and her teacher, Anne Sullivan, it was the word and the substance that changed their lives.

Born in Alabama to wealthy parents, Helen began life like any other child. But before her second birthday, a terrible illness robbed her of sight and hearing. Suddenly, this bright, curious little girl lived in a world without light or sound. Although Helen tried to communicate using signs she invented herself, she knew that other people did many, many things that she could not. And it made her angry.

As Helen grew older, she grew angrier. She would explode into kicking, screaming temper tantrums every day. Her parents desperately wanted to help her, but they didn't know how. Then Anne Sullivan came into their lives. A teacher from a school for the blind, she moved in with Helen's family, determined to improve Helen's life. Anne was strict but caring. She encouraged Helen to use her remaining senses to experience the world around her. She taught her to spell words with her fingers (*water* was the first), recognize objects by touch, and read

Helen Keller (*left*) and Anne Sullivan are pictured around 1897, when Helen was still a teen. Later, Helen was to become the first deaf-blind person to graduate from college. Throughout those years, Anne Sullivan laboriously spelled books and lectures into her pupil's hand.

Braille. Helen even learned to speak.

Now Helen wanted to try *everything*. She rode horses, swam, took walks in the woods, and learned to row a boat. She graduated with honors from Radcliffe, a prestigious college for women. She wrote and lectured about being deaf and blind. Helen had found her way out of the darkness.

For forty years, Helen Keller and Anne Sullivan traveled around the world, helping

"I knew then that 'w-a-t-e-r' meant the wonderful cool something that was flowing over my hand. That living word awakened my soul, gave it light, hope, joy, set it free!" —*Helen Keller*

to raise awareness about the lives of people with disabilities. Presidents invited Keller to the White House. Foreign governments showered her with honors. When Anne Sullivan died in 1936, Helen Keller mourned the passing of her friend but continued to travel and inspire.

Helen Keller was eighty-seven years old when she died in 1968. She never saw the audiences who marveled at her abilities and her spirit. She never heard their applause. She only felt their love and respect.

DIVE IN!

Helen Keller: An Impulse to Soar by Caitie McAneney (PowerKids Press, 2021), 32 pages.

Helen's Eyes: A Photobiography of Annie Sullivan, Helen Keller's Teacher by Marfe Ferguson Delano (National Geographic Children's Books, 2015), 64 pages.

EXPLORE!

How easily can people with vision or hearing impairments find their way around your school or neighborhood? To learn more about improving accessibility for everyone, visit the Helen Keller National Center (HKNC) for DeafBlind Youths and Adults at www.hknc.org.

You can read about helping deaf-blind people manage in a seeing and hearing world. Explore their website, and then check out your own environment. Does your town have beeping traffic lights? Are elevators equipped with Braille numbers? Does your school teach anything about sign language or Seeing Eye dogs? Did you know that you can raise a puppy to become a Seeing Eye dog? Visit www.seeingeye.org to learn about the oldest guide dog school in the world.

EXPLORE SOME MORE!

Watch the movie *The Miracle Worker*. You may choose from a few versions of the film. You'll cringe when Helen explodes into fits of rage. You'll cheer when she realizes that objects have names that you can spell with your fingers. You'll see young Helen learn the significance of "w-a-t-e-r." The movie's title came from American author Mark Twain, who used the phrase to describe Anne Sullivan. Don't miss this classic story!

Helen Keller poses with one of her dogs.

THE REVEREND
DR. MARTIN
LUTHER KING JR.

JANUARY 15, 1929–APRIL 4, 1968

THE VOICE OF EQUALITY
**CIVIL RIGHTS LEADER
MINISTER
HUMANITARIAN
NOBEL PEACE PRIZE WINNER
AUTHOR**

Would you let angry people throw tin cans and rocks and rotten **eggs at you?** Would you let a powerful fire hose spray water on you and knock you down, bruising and hurting you? Would you let dogs bite you? Would you tolerate any of these things and not fight back?

The children of Birmingham, Alabama, endured all these things because they believed in the powerful words of the Reverend Dr. Martin Luther King Jr. Still powerful today, in the 1960s they were the words that made most Americans realize that racism had to end. You probably think we mean most *adult* Americans. No, we mean kids too.

Dr. King was arrested on Good Friday 1963. He spent one of the Christian world's major holy days, Easter Sunday, alone in a jail cell. There, he wrote a famous letter, explaining why the civil rights protesters must fight hate with love. The city was filled with racial hate, and children wanted to be part of the protests. Should he allow them, knowing that some of them could get hurt?

For three nights after his release from jail he

On December 10, 1964, Martin Luther King Jr. received the Nobel Peace Prize. More than fifty years later, his acceptance speech still rings with hope. "I accept this award on behalf of a civil rights movement which is moving with determination and a majestic scorn for risk and danger to establish a reign of freedom and a rule of justice."

lay awake, trying to decide. Eventually, he knew the answer. "The children and grandchildren are doing it for themselves." They should take part.

And so, when Birmingham's marches for equality and justice resumed, there they were. First, teenage girls, then elementary school children, then high school boys joining in the protests. Horrible things happened to them. Hundreds were arrested. And all of it was seen on television. A horrified United States saw

"Hate cannot drive out hate, only love can do that."

—Martin Luther King Jr.

the ugly face of racism against children. And Americans finally realized that the time had come to listen to the words of Martin Luther King Jr.

EXPLORE!

Few people in our country's brief history (remember, we are a young nation by history's standards) have been as powerful with words as was Dr. King. His speeches helped to bring alive our Declaration of Independence's key phrase: ". . . all men are created equal."

Read a portion of his famous "I Have a Dream" speech, proclaimed on August 28, 1963, at the Lincoln Memorial—or, better yet, listen to it. You can find it easily on YouTube. You'll understand why, as a nation, we have honored Dr. King with a national holiday—January 15, his birthday. You'll understand why, in 1964, he was awarded the Nobel Peace Prize.

Visit the King Center at www.thekingcenter .org. There you will find mountains of information about the man and his work.

At www.nps.gov/malu, you can explore the Martin Luther King Jr. National

Historical Park in Georgia. Another website, www.nps.gov/mlkm, will let you explore the Martin Luther King Jr. Memorial in Washington, DC. This statue was unveiled in 2011 after nearly two decades of planning.

EXPLORE SOME MORE!

A truly wonderful tradition has evolved to honor Dr. King on his birthday. It is the annual Martin Luther King Jr. Day of Service! Find out what is happening on that day in your community. Since Martin Luther King Jr. Day is a national holiday and your school will be closed, you can participate. Search online for the MLK Jr. Day of Service, and read about many ways you can help others and honor Dr. King. Visit https://tocaboca.com/magazine/community-service-ideas-for-kids-and-families-mlk-day for more.

DIVE IN!

I See the Promised Land: A Life of Martin Luther King Jr. by Arthur Flowers (Tara Books, 2013), 154 pages.

On August 28, 1963, Martin Luther King Jr. *(center left)* and other civil rights leaders came together in the nation's capital for the March on Washington for Jobs and Freedom.

MERIWETHER LEWIS, WILLIAM CLARK, AND SACAGAWEA

LEWIS: AUGUST 18, 1774–OCTOBER 11, 1809

CLARK: AUGUST 1, 1770–SEPTEMBER 1, 1838

SACAGAWEA: CA. 1786–CA. 1812 OR 1884

TRAILBLAZERS
EXPLORERS

It was one of the greatest bargains of all time. For a mere $15 million, President Thomas Jefferson bought the entire Louisiana Territory from the French Empire under Napoleon. The United States was the proud owner of 828,000 square miles (2,144,510 sq. km).

To find out about our new addition, President Jefferson sent army captains Meriwether Lewis and William Clark, along with thirty-one soldiers, on an expedition to explore the land from the Northern Great Plains (around Saint Louis, Missouri) to the Pacific Ocean. This "Corps of Discovery" faced two years and four months of blizzards and bears, floods and hunger, illness and uncertainty. Survival depended upon their ingenuity and ability to live off the land.

For all their skill and courage, Lewis and Clark would probably have had an even harder time without a young Shoshone woman named Sacagawea (sometimes spelled Sacajawea). She was a teenager and pregnant when the explorers hired her French-born husband to help guide

Portraits of William Clark *(top)* and Meriwether Lewis *(bottom)*

their expedition west. Throughout the journey, she served as interpreter, negotiated for horses when the explorers needed them, added to the travelers' diet with roots and plants, and showed incredible strength and courage. She and her newborn son, traveling with thirty-three men, also served as a symbol of peace to the Native tribes they encountered along the way.

"... as no woman ever accompanies a war party of Indians in this quarter. A woman with a party of men is a token of peace." —*William Clark (from his journal)*

This venture into the West opened new chapters in our nation's history. The team of Lewis, Clark, and Sacagawea had indeed blazed a new trail.

EXPLORE!

True or false: the expedition of Lewis and Clark and Sacagawea was of immense benefit to the peoples of North America. You're right! It's a trick question.

Our country was still very young, and white settlers were eager to move and acquire new land. But the land they wanted was already inhabited by Native Americans. So the Lewis and Clark Expedition clearly brought different results for different people. The positive consequences for one group were negative consequences for another.

To encourage you to think about these heroes and this historical dilemma, we want you to start a journal. That's what Lewis and Clark did during their travels. Find a book or website such as https://lewisandclarkjournals.unl.edu/ where you can read the explorers' journal entries. You'll need some accurate background to get a feel for the time period and setting. In your journal, imagine the lives of different people involved in the expedition.

One of the ways we can bring great historical people to life is by "walking a mile in their shoes." Your journal will help you do that. We would like to read some of your journal, if you don't mind sharing. It would be interesting to see how different kids in different parts of the country view the journeys of Lewis, Clark, and Sacagawea.

This statue of Sacagawea and her son stands in North Dakota. Some historians think that she died when she was twenty-five. However, according to Shoshoni oral history, Sacagawea lived a much longer life, calling herself Porivo. Porivo died at the age of ninety-six.

Not sure how to get started? Search for "journal ideas for kids" on the internet. Sometimes these ideas are called "prompts." You might find prompts like these: What is your favorite holiday? What is the best/worst thing about September?

EXPLORE SOME MORE!

Go to https://www.nps.gov/lecl /learn/kidsyouth/index.htm, and become a Lewis and Clark Junior Ranger!

DIVE IN!

The Lewis and Clark Expedition by Beatrice Harris (Gareth Stevens, 2022), 32 pages.

Sacagawea by Lise Erdrich (Carolrhoda Books, 2003), 40 pages.

ABRAHAM LINCOLN

FEBRUARY 12, 1809–APRIL 15, 1865

THE GREAT EMANCIPATOR
US PRESIDENT
ORATOR
LEGEND

Compassionate, courageous, strong, brilliant, determined, honest— heroic words come easily to mind when we think about Abraham Lincoln. His face and profile are probably the most recognized of any American hero. Close your eyes and you can picture him immediately. Honest Abe is as much a part of all of us as is our flag, the Fourth of July, the Statue of Liberty, and our fifty states. He's the man who ended slavery and saved the Union.

Since you've probably already learned more at school about Abraham Lincoln than most of the other heroes, we'll try to tell you something about him you might not already know. He was the first US president to grow a beard. And it's all because of a letter from an eleven-year-old girl.

Grace Bedell lived in Westfield, New York. Shortly before the election of 1860, when the country was having real trouble because of the slavery issue, she wrote to candidate Lincoln with some advice. She told him that growing a beard would help him win because ". . . you would look a great deal better for your face is so thin. All the ladies like whiskers and they would tease their husbands to vote for you." *

*Women were not allowed to vote in 1860. Another of our 60 American heroes helped change that. Do you know who she is?

Abraham Lincoln had great public success, but his personal life was filled with tragedy. Only one of his four sons lived to maturity.

Well, Lincoln took young Grace's advice. It's doubtful his decision to grow a beard made a difference in the voting. Remember, there was no TV or online news to announce "Lincoln Grows Beard!" But her influence did certainly change how everyone from 1860 to the present day remembers and pictures Abraham Lincoln. Isn't it amazing the difference a simple letter can make?

We hope you know that the Power Words on page 75 are found at the end of the Gettysburg Address, one of the most famous speeches ever given. President Lincoln wrote the speech and delivered it on November 19, 1863, in

Gettysburg, Pennsylvania. The entire speech lasted only two minutes! Do you know how the speech begins?

EXPLORE!

It's been said that where someone grows up can have a huge effect on how they live their life. Abe Lincoln grew up in a log cabin, with many challenges and none of the conveniences that we take for granted today. What was it like to live in a log cabin in the early 1800s? Was there heat? Did the cabin have windows? Beds? Books? Do some digging online and make a list of the ways that Lincoln's boyhood home was different from yours. Make a model or draw pictures as you learn. Then figure out how Abe's early life led him to become a lawyer, an orator, and president of the United States. Use your imagination!

Dig into the books written about him and the tons of Lincoln-related websites on the internet. Uncover incidents from his life that show his compassion and courage. As you read these stories, you'll discover something about the legendary man. You'll discover that President Lincoln was a real human being. Each story you find will help you appreciate how genuinely good he was. You'll see

DIVE IN!

Abraham Lincoln: The Gettysburg Address by Rebecca Sjonger (Crabtree, 2019), 48 pages.

him as a legend. You'll see him as a human being. You'll see him as an example of how you can live your life.

EXPLORE SOME MORE!

The most famous monument ever built to honor Abe Lincoln is probably the Lincoln Memorial. You can see it if you visit Washington, DC, but if you can't, you'll find it at www.nps.gov/linc. It's an awesome tribute to an awesome man. The monument is made of marble and granite.

The Lincoln Memorial includes a statue of Lincoln that is 19 feet (6 m) high, as well as carved inscriptions from his Gettysburg Address and his second inaugural address.

POWER WORDS!

". . . and that government of the people, by the people, for the people shall not perish from the earth."

—*Abraham Lincoln*

YO-YO MA

OCTOBER 7, 1955–

THE WORLD'S FINEST CELLIST
MUSICIAN
EDUCATOR
MUSICAL AMBASSADOR

Yo-Yo Ma in 2005

Music. It's almost everywhere. You dance to it, march to it, worship through it, celebrate with it . . . and many of you make it—you are musicians. Meet one of the world's greatest musicians—Yo-Yo Ma.

Can you remember what you were doing when you were five years old? Yo-Yo Ma was giving his first public cello recital. That's right, at the age you were singing "The Wheels on the Bus" in kindergarten, he was playing an instrument in front of an audience. A cello, by the way, is a stringed instrument, larger than a violin but smaller than a string bass.

Yo-Yo Ma has become a world-famous ambassador for classical music. He travels everywhere and plays with great orchestras and other famous musicians. He has made more than one hundred albums. Eighteen of them have been honored with Grammy Awards.

He is always trying to find new and different ways to reach more people with classical music. In the early 1990s, Yo-Yo Ma teamed up with Bobby McFerrin for a pretty unusual performance in Boston. McFerrin is a jazz musician who uses his voice as an instrument. The pair teamed up with the Boston Philharmonic and put together a concert of all kinds of music—classical, fun, mournful, and lighthearted. They also recorded *Hush*, an album that you can listen to online.

And Yo-Yo Ma does not think classical music is just for grown-ups either. He has taken his cello to *Sesame Street* and *Mister Rogers' Neighborhood*. Whenever he goes on a concert tour, he schedules time to teach students, both musicians and nonmusicians. He also encourages young people to create music, and he teaches them how. He has been known to share his instruments with them. The cellos that Ma plays are very valuable, worth hundreds of thousands, even *millions* of dollars. But on more than one occasion, he has invited young cello students to experience the thrill of playing one of his practically priceless instruments. This is what Yo-Yo Ma does. He loves music so much that he wants to share it with the world.

"Music connects human beings. It brings people together." —*Yo-Yo Ma*

Yo-Yo Ma loves to play and create new music. Here he performs at the National Gallery of Art on April 20, 2015.

EXPLORE!

Music can build bridges of understanding between cultures. In many ways, it is the truest international language. We can enjoy a song even if we don't understand the words. Yo-Yo Ma's talents are so special because each time he draws his bow across the strings of his cello, he reaches across cultures, across generations, across types of music. He makes music universal. Listen to his music on www.yo-yoma.com. As you enjoy his extraordinary performance, think of the many types of music you probably have never listened to. Then look for some. We want you to explore music from other cultures. Look around online for new and interesting types of music. Or ask your friends who have a different cultural background to share their music.

Then listen. Really listen. Why? Because appreciating the music of others helps you

DIVE IN!

Yo-Yo Ma: Grammy Award-Winning Cellist by Jeanne Nagel and Lisa A. Chippendale (Enslow, 2017), 128 pages.

to appreciate them as well. Understanding and tolerance begin by learning to see that "different is okay." Different music—from whatever culture—is okay, just different. Different people—from whatever culture—are OK, just different. Simple.

So begin letting Yo-Yo Ma's beautiful music lead you to be more accepting of everybody's music. And of everybody.

EXPLORE SOME MORE!

Did you know that during the COVID-19 pandemic Yo-Yo Ma and his colleague Emanuel Ax performed concerts for frontline workers such as EMTs, doctors and nurses, teachers, delivery workers, and others? Yo-Yo Ma is committed to using music to heal and inspire. Visit www.silkroadproject.org to learn about another amazing music project that he started. You may even want to get involved!

GEORGE C. MARSHALL

DECEMBER 31, 1880–OCTOBER 16, 1959

ARCHITECT OF PEACE
**ARMY CHIEF OF STAFF
SECRETARY OF STATE
NOBEL PEACE PRIZE WINNER**

President Harry S. Truman called General George C. Marshall "the greatest of the great of our time." High praise, but do you even know who George C. Marshall was?

In 1953, for the first time ever, the Nobel Peace Prize was given to a professional soldier. Why? Because General George C. Marshall came up with a plan that saved war-torn Europe from starvation and despair after World War II. Whole cities and towns had been destroyed. Bridges, roads, homes, and schools were gone. Two years after the war, Europe was still having trouble getting back on its feet. The Marshall Plan would offer US aid for recovery, but not only to our World War II allies. We would help our former enemies too, if they let us.

Don't miss this point: for the first time ever in the history of the world, the victors offered to help the vanquished! In a speech at Harvard University on June 6, 1947, Marshall said: "[Without] the return of normal economic health in the world . . . there can be no political stability and no assured peace." He continued: "Our policy is directed not against any country or doctrine, but against hunger, poverty, desperation, and chaos." Marshall knew that if things went on as they were, hungry Europeans would look for help elsewhere, even if their helper gave food

George C. Marshall became chief of staff of the US Army on September 1, 1939. It was the same day Nazi Germany invaded Poland, initiating World War II.

with one hand and took freedom and justice away with the other. If they had to turn to Eastern Europe's Communist dictators for aid, that's exactly what would have happened.

Well, the Marshall Plan worked. Our enemies refused help (they didn't want to play by our rules), but the rest of Europe recovered and peace prevailed. Years later, when he accepted his Nobel Prize, the frail, seventy-three-year-old general spoke of democracy's greatness but warned that these democratic principles "do not flourish on empty stomachs."

"There must be an effort of the spirit—to be magnanimous, to act in friendship, to strive to help rather than to hinder."

—General George C. Marshall (in a lecture given on the day after he accepted the Nobel Peace Prize in 1953)

EXPLORE!

One of the world's greatest honors is to be awarded the Nobel Prize for Peace. To date, twenty-one Americans have been so honored; seven of them are found in this book: Marshall, Jane Addams, Jimmy Carter, the Reverend Dr. Martin Luther King Jr., Barack Obama, Theodore Roosevelt, and Elie Wiesel. Use the internet or library reference section to find the names of the other winners.

Did you know that Nobel Prize winners receive a cash award? Jane Addams gave hers to the Women's International League for Peace and Freedom. Dr. King donated his $54,600 prize to the civil rights movement. Roosevelt distributed his prize to various charities, and Elie Wiesel founded the Elie Wiesel Foundation for Humanity with the $290,000 he received from the Nobel Committee. No one is quite sure what George Marshall did with his prize money of $33,840, not even the researchers at the George C. Marshall Foundation, an organization dedicated to "preserving and promoting . . . the ideals and values of disciplined selfless service, hard work, integrity and compassion of George Catlett Marshall." Check out the George C. Marshall Foundation at www.marshallfoundation.org.

When President Obama won the Nobel Peace Prize, he was awarded $1.4 million, which he gave to charity. What would you do with the money if you won the peace prize? Would you use it to promote peace? How? Send us your ideas at https://heroes4us.com/contact-american-heroes/.

DIVE IN!

Fighting Wars, Planning for Peace: The Story of George C. Marshall by Lee Gimpel (Morgan Reynolds Pub., 2005), 176 pages.

Marshall (*right*) shakes hands with President Truman at an awards ceremony on November 26, 1945.

JOHN MUIR

APRIL 21, 1838–DECEMBER 24, 1914

FATHER OF OUR NATIONAL PARKS
CONSERVATIONIST
AUTHOR
NATURALIST

Even as a boy, John Muir loved **nature.** Plants and animals fascinated him. His first glimpse of lightning bugs after the family came to the United States from Scotland was thrilling. However, John was also a practical, hardworking person. After attending college for a while, he was not sure what he wanted to do with his life. He was a "tinkerer"—an inventor. Maybe he would create new machines.

One day, while he was working in a factory, a sharp piece of a metal file flew into his right eye. Suddenly, he was blinded. Within a few hours, his entire world was dark. For a month, Muir faced a future of total uncertainty. Then, amazingly, his sight returned. What he regained was more than his eye vision. John Muir found his life's vision. "God has to nearly kill us sometimes to teach us lessons," he said. The wilderness—that was where Muir really wanted to be. Not in a factory in some city. But in nature, exploring and learning everything he could.

All of us have benefited from John Muir's transformation. As he traveled, he became the champion of preserving the magnificent places we now value as our national parks.

EXPLORE!
John Muir's favorite place was Yosemite, a beautiful California landscape of mountains

As a wilderness explorer, John Muir was known for his solo excursions in California's Sierra Nevada region, among Alaska's glaciers, and to Australia, South America, Africa, Europe, China, Japan, or anywhere in the world that would afford him the opportunity to bask in the unspoiled beauty of nature.

and waterfalls. Saving it to be one of our great national parks is part of his legacy. But he also *lost* a conservation battle—a battle to save the equally beautiful Hetch Hetchy Valley, part of the Yosemite region. The website www.hetchhetchy.org tells the story of this river that was dammed to provide San Francisco with water. Now, nearly one hundred years later, John Muir's struggle is being refought. And you can join in.

Why bother? Because someday, you may be lucky enough to visit Yosemite and maybe see Hetch Hetchy too. And even if you don't, you'll know that your voice joined others in letting decision makers know what the United States wants. That's what our country is all about—every citizen, young or old, being heard.

EXPLORE SOME MORE!

In 1892 John Muir started the Sierra Club. Visit its website at www.sierraclub.org to learn about its values and causes. Then visit the US National Park Service website: www.nps.gov. It shows how amazing our national parks are. Think about visiting them and imagine yourself working as a national park ranger someday.

DIVE IN!

John Muir: America's First Environmentalist by Kathryn Lasky (Candlewick, 2014), 45 pages.

POWER WORDS!

"Whenever we try to pick out anything by itself, we find it hitched to everything else in the universe." —*John Muir*

In 1901 Muir wrote *Our National Parks*, the book that brought him to the attention of President Theodore Roosevelt. In 1903 Roosevelt (*left*) visited Muir in Yosemite. It was there that they collaborated on what were to become Roosevelt's innovative conservation programs.

BARACK OBAMA

AUGUST 4, 1961–

US PRESIDENT
FIRST BLACK PRESIDENT
NOBEL PEACE PRIZE WINNER
AUTHOR

It is the most important phrase in the Declaration of Independence: "All men [meaning all people] are created equal." What a noble ideal. But the United States, like every country in the world, past and present, often struggles to line up with its ideals.

Throughout US history, schoolchildren have been told that anyone can grow up to be president. But for the longest time, only white men were elected to the highest office in the land. That changed in the historic election of 2008, when Barack Obama tore down the barriers and took his place as the forty-fourth president of the United States. That election forever changed the face of American leadership.

President Obama's personal history is a fascinating story that unfolded in locations around the world. He was born in Hawaii (the only president of Hawaiian birth) to a white mother from Kansas and a Black father from Kenya. They were both students at the University of Hawaii when they met. Soon after Barack was born, his father left the family.

Barack and his mother moved often during his formative years. They spent time in Washington, Indonesia, and Hawaii. Wherever he lived, Barack kept up with his schoolwork. Education was of great importance to his family, and it paved the way for his success. His mother also continued to learn, and she would eventually earn a PhD in anthropology.

Barack Obama ran a brilliant presidential campaign in 2008. Four years later, he was elected to a second term as chief executive of the United States.

Barack was an outstanding student. In 1983 he graduated from Columbia University with a degree in political science. Eight years later, he earned a law degree from Harvard University, where he graduated magna cum laude, which means "with great honor." He has written that his blended cultural upbringing and commitment to education shaped many of the ideas and values that guided him as president.

EXPLORE!

Three simple words—"Yes, we can"—became the most popular slogan for Barack Obama's historic

"Yes, we can." —*Barack Obama*

DIVE IN!

Barack Obama: Our 44th President by Beatrice Gormley (Aladdin, 2015), 266 pages.

campaign in 2008. He used that powerful, confident phrase twelve times during his New Hampshire primary speech. Read the speech online, and each time you come to the words "Yes, we can," say them out loud. That declaration, along with the word *hope*, defined his successful presidential run.

Did President Obama make things happen in his eight years in office? Did "Yes, we can" become "Yes, we did"? Grading a president's performance is what historians do. We want you to become a historian and give the president a grade. That means digging for evidence by reading about the actions Obama took in office.

Barack Obama and his family greet an excited crowd in Chicago, Illinois, on November 4, 2008, after his presidential election victory.

1) Read the Dive In! book on this page and research the Obama presidency online. List five major issues you want to explore.
2) Read more about those issues. Write down key phrases and ideas, and think about their meanings.
3) Talk with adults about your research. To get a wide range of opinions, talk to people who agreed and disagreed with President Obama about certain issues.
4) Weigh the evidence and make a judgment.

Assign President Obama a final grade, and explain how you reached your decision.

EXPLORE SOME MORE!

The mission of the Obama Foundation is "to inspire, empower, and connect people to change their world." Visit https://www.obama.org to learn more about this dynamic organization and how you can get involved. Then go to https://www.obama.org/mbka to explore the My Brother's Keeper Alliance, an initiative to help "boys and young men of color and to ensure all youth can reach their full potential." Share the information with adults in your life. Together, talk about how you can make your community a safe and supportive place for everyone. What other Obama Foundation initiatives make you say, "Yes, we can"?

SANDRA DAY O'CONNOR

MARCH 26, 1930–

FIRST WOMAN US SUPREME COURT JUSTICE

SUPREME COURT JUSTICE
LAWYER
AUTHOR

Justice O'Connor shattered the idea that women were not qualified to serve on the Supreme Court—and as a role model, further opened the door for women at all levels of the legal profession.

What's it like to be the first to do something? Maybe you were the first in your family to learn to tap dance. Maybe you were the first among your friends to learn to snowboard. If so, then you're like Sandra Day O'Connor, the first woman ever appointed to the US Supreme Court, the most important group of judges in the country.

Being the first isn't always the easiest way to go. If you're the first, you must be able to handle all the responsibilities and all of the problems that go with it. When she first became a lawyer, law firms in San Francisco and Los Angeles rejected Sandra Day O'Connor. She was a woman, and the legal world wasn't used to women in the courtroom. It didn't matter how good or smart she was. But O'Connor persisted, and her persistence paid off. Becoming the first woman on the highest court in the land represented acceptance and a step for all women on the road to equal rights.

Oh, there's one more important "first" in Justice O'Connor's lifetime of firsts. Her family. She did the juggling of career, home, and kids that many moms today have to do. She was a full-time mother for a while when her three boys were very young. Then, when she resumed the practice of law, she established priorities,

and commitment to family remained at the top of the list. Though history will surely focus on her accomplishments in Washington, DC, we shouldn't only admire her for her Supreme Court job. Justice O'Connor is a wife, a mother, a grandmother, a citizen, a person—and a terrific role model—a hero.

Although she loved serving on the Supreme Court, Justice O'Connor retired in 2006. Why? She stayed home to care for her husband, who had Alzheimer's disease. Family first—nothing could stop her from honoring that commitment.

EXPLORE!

To many Americans, the US Supreme Court is a mysterious place. The magnificent building across the street from the US Capitol is open to the public, but few people visit it. Why? Maybe because we think of courtrooms as boring. There certainly aren't any airplanes hanging from the ceiling as in Washington's Air and Space Museum. Or maybe we think that what goes on in the Supreme Court's courtroom doesn't really affect our lives. Wrong!

The Supreme Court makes our Constitution

Sandra Day O'Connor retired from the Supreme Court in 2006.

a "living document." The justices interpret that 1787 document and apply it to our lives. Today. The Supreme Court's official website (www.supremecourt.gov) has some cool information to share. Go to the tab titled "About the Court" and click on "Justices" and then "Current Members" to find out more about Sandra Day O'Connor (she is still listed there even though she is retired), Chief Justice John G. Roberts Jr., and the other justices. You can also examine actual Supreme Court decisions, read oral arguments and case documents, learn about the rules of the court, and much more.

Visit the Supreme Court's website often to keep track of what's on the docket (what cases the justices are discussing), and keep an eye on the news. Something the justices rule on today could affect you in a big way tomorrow. The law is *real*, and the way judges interpret it can change your life. Pay attention!

DIVE IN!

Lazy B: Growing up on a Cattle Ranch in the American Southwest by Sandra Day O'Connor and H. Alan Day (Random House, 2002), 318 pages.

POWER WORDS!

"Whether your future work is in business, in government, or as a volunteer, try to set your sights on doing something worthwhile and then work hard at it."

—*Justice Sandra Day O'Connor*

JESSE OWENS

SEPTEMBER 12, 1913–MARCH 31, 1980

OLYMPIC LEGEND
ATHLETE
HUMANITARIAN
AUTHOR

Jesse Owens runs during the 1936 Olympic Games in Berlin, Germany.

Legends are created in many different ways. Jesse Owens became an international hero by overcoming bias to triumph on the world's biggest sports stage.

Owens first showed his athletic potential as an amazing high school track-and-field star in Cleveland, Ohio. Many colleges recruited him for his incredible running and jumping abilities. Owens chose the Ohio State University Buckeyes of the Big Ten conference. He earned a nickname at the school that stayed with him his whole life: Buckeye Bullet.

Just before the 1935 Big Ten Outdoor Track and Field Championships, Owens fell down some stairs and hurt his back. He wasn't sure he could compete, but he decided to give it a try. What happened next was "the greatest single day performance in athletic history," according to *Sports Illustrated*. Owens tied the world record in the 100-yard dash. Then he set a new world long-jump record ten minutes later. Within the next thirty minutes or so, he also set new world records in the 220-yard dash and the 220-yard low hurdles. Owens had tied or set new world records in four events in just forty-five minutes!

Owens's performance at the 1935 Big Ten Championships was incredible, but it was the 1936 Summer Olympics in Berlin, Germany, that made him a legend. Twenty-two-year-old Owens was one of just eighteen Black athletes on the United States Olympic team. He was looking to add Olympic gold to the collection of collegiate honors already on display in his trophy case.

Throngs of fans were eager to see him and get his autograph, including many young German fans. Owens needed police escorts to make his way around town. His popularity in Nazi Germany was surprising—the country's

POWER WORDS!

"We all have dreams. But in order to make dreams come into reality, it takes an awful lot of determination, dedication, self-discipline, and effort." —*Jesse Owens*

leaders simmered with hatred and racism. Germany's leader, Adolf Hitler, hoped that the Olympics would promote his belief that non-Jewish white people, referred to as Aryans, were a master race and superior to people of all other races. The Olympics were meant to be a propaganda showpiece for white superiority.

That was the plan, until Jesse Owens started running and jumping. He captured four gold medals: the long jump, the 100-meter dash, the 200-meter dash, and the 4x100-meter relay. Four gold medals in a single Olympics had never before been accomplished by a track-and-field athlete, and it was a record that stood for forty-eight years.

Owens had been a celebrated athlete before he traveled to Berlin for the 1936 Olympics. But his appearance in Hitler's Germany made him forever a legend in Olympic history.

EXPLORE!

Read Jesse Owens's Power Words carefully. They serve as a reminder of how ordinary people reach extraordinary goals.

Heroes start with a dream, a mental vision of what they want to accomplish. Then they begin the hard work needed to make that dream become real. Owens's words apply to areas other than sports. A person can dream of accomplishments in science, medicine, music, art, writing, environmental protection—there is no limit to what you can dream! Whatever you hope to accomplish, Owens's four-step formula applies: have the *determination* to set a

DIVE IN!

Jesse Owens by Heather Williams (Cherry Lake, 2019), 32 pages.

goal, the *dedication* to do your best, and the *self-discipline* to keep on trying. Combine all of this with a ton of *effort*, and you'll achieve your dream.

What is your number one dream? Regardless of your age, you can begin to focus on how you will make your dream come true. To help you stay on track, post Owens's Power Words in your bedroom. Memorize them and share them with friends and family, or just keep the words to yourself for inspiration.

Owens was the son of sharecroppers and the grandson of enslaved people. Yet his name and his achievements and his legend live on because he made his dream come true through determination, dedication, self-discipline, and effort. So can YOU!

EXPLORE SOME MORE!

After retiring from track and field, Owens spent a lot of time speaking to youth groups to inspire them to greatness. In 1976 he was honored for his Olympic triumphs and humanitarian service with the Presidential Medal of Freedom. Use the internet to learn more about Owen's accomplishments on and off the track.

Jesse Owens (center) on the medal stand after winning the long jump competition at the 1936 Olympics

ROSA PARKS

FEBRUARY 4, 1913–OCTOBER 24, 2005

MOTHER OF THE CIVIL RIGHTS MOVEMENT
CIVIL RIGHTS ACTIVIST
AUTHOR

Did you ever drop a pebble into a pool of water? The pebble makes waves, watery circles hundreds of times larger than the pebble itself. You might call Rosa Parks a kind of "pebble dropper." She is a Black woman who, on December 1, 1955, refused to give up her seat on a city bus to a white man. That simple deed created waves that reached way beyond the Parks's home in Montgomery, Alabama. She had tossed a pebble that would change the pool forever.

Back in the 1950s, many states including Alabama kept Jim Crow laws on the books. These laws kept white people and Black people apart in almost all public areas, including city buses. White people were allowed to sit in the front, and Black people had to go to the back of the bus, to the "colored" section. If more white people boarded the bus, then Black people had to stand and give their seats in the back to the whites. Everyone followed the rules. It was the law. But Rosa Parks broke the law.

On that day, this hardworking seamstress said no when the bus driver ordered her to give up her seat. She had worked all day, and she was tired. Too tired to walk home as she usually did to avoid the indignity of the segregated bus. More important, though, was the other kind of tired she felt. She was tired of giving in. So she didn't. Parks believed that the question of where to sit on the bus was not a little thing. The angry bus driver didn't think it was a little

Rosa Parks sits near the front of a bus in Montgomery, Alabama, in 1956.

thing either. He called the police, and Rosa Parks was arrested.

Was she scared? Of course she was. She knew how Black people were treated in the city jails. But she knew it was time to take a stand for what she believed was right.

Rosa Parks understood the meaning of the words in both the Declaration of Independence and the Constitution. It was time to make the words about equality work for every American. This courageous woman's simple deed led to a major boycott of city buses in Montgomery. It would soon become the rallying point for the civil rights movement that was just beginning to attract attention. Rosa Parks's simple act of courage was going to change the United States.

EXPLORE!

A single, simple act of courage. For Rosa Parks, it was simply refusing to give up her seat. For teenager Ryan White, it was simply refusing to hide from those who viciously discriminated against him because he had AIDS. Instead, he chose to teach the world about the disease that would claim his life. For Temple Grandin, it was refusing to allow people to discriminate against her because of her autism, a condition that affects the ways she interacts with the world. Temple was teased and bullied when she was young, but with her parents' support, she discovered her talents and became a nationally known author and speaker on autism and animal behavior. Search online for more about Ryan White and Temple Grandin.

Do you know any stories like theirs? Tell us about someone who stood tall when things were rough. Zero in on people who have battled discrimination and hatred, such as Rosa Parks and Ryan White. The people you tell us about may be famous, but they don't have to be. Scan your own family, community, or school for single acts of courage. Tell us about the dance teacher who stopped kids from bullying the boys who wanted to dance. Or the aunt and uncle who talked you and your friends out of bad-mouthing kids from another neighborhood.

POWER WORDS!

> "Some people think I kept my seat because I'd had a hard day, but that is not true. I was just tired of giving in." —*Rosa Parks*

Rosa Parks is fingerprinted at the police station after being arrested in Montgomery. A Supreme Court decision would later strike down the long-ingrained practice of racial segregation on public transportation.

EXPLORE SOME MORE!

We're challenging you to go on a search. In 2013 an amazing statue of Rosa Parks was unveiled. It was the first life-size statue of a Black woman to be placed in this building. Look online to discover where the statue is and read the story of its dedication.

DIVE IN!

The Rebellious Life of Mrs. Rosa Parks by Jeanne Theoharis (Beacon Press, 2021), 296 pages.

DOLLY PARTON

JANUARY 19, 1946–

MUSIC LEGEND
SONGWRITER AND SINGER
AUTHOR
ACTOR
BUSINESSPERSON
PHILANTHROPIST

I will always love you." Dolly Parton wrote those lyrics and recorded them in a song of the same name in 1974. The words sum up exactly how her millions of fans feel about this talented person.

Parton knew when she was a little girl that she wanted to be a superstar. Possessing a ton of talent and confidence, she built her career through hard work and dedication.

Family played the most important role in shaping Dolly Parton. She was the fourth of twelve children, all raised in a small log cabin in the Great Smoky Mountains of Tennessee. The family was poor, and the cabin had no electricity and no running water. In her song "Coat of Many Colors," she captures the love and joy she experienced as a child despite the family's poverty.

Parton began to sing professionally when she was only ten years old, appearing on local TV and radio shows. At thirteen, she performed at the Grand Ole Opry in Nashville, Tennessee, a famous showcase for country music talent. In 1967 Parton joined country music star Porter Wagoner's TV show, *The Porter Wagoner Show*, where she refined her music skills and made important connections in the music business.

Eventually, Parton struck out on her own. Her life became a whirlwind of writing, performing hit songs, and acting in movies. She

Dolly Parton performs in Louisville, Kentucky. She has sold more than one hundred million albums to music fans around the world.

opened Dollywood (a theme park in Tennessee), started her own music publishing company, and won many awards.

Parton kept receiving honors in the 2000s. In 2006 she received the Kennedy Center Honors, a *huge* award given to the best of the best in the performing arts. And in 2019, she celebrated her fiftieth year with the Grand Old Opry! You can learn more about the Opry at https://www.opry.com. While her rise to fame was mainly in country music, she became so much more to millions of fans around the world.

Parton still lives in the Tennessee mountains with her husband, Carl Dean, and she has a deep connection with the community. She has donated money to important causes, including to wildfire relief in Tennessee and COVID-19 research. She also supports reading and education through Dolly Parton's Imagination Library.

Parton never abandoned her country roots, and that's one reason she's still so popular with fans. No one in the entertainment business is more beloved than Parton!

EXPLORE!

Dolly Parton's Imagination Library—that's a catchy title. But you should know it is filled with more than imagination. The library is full of real books meant for kids all over the United States and the world.

In 1995 Parton started to give away free books to kids in her Tennessee community. Her father never learned how to read, partly because he didn't have access to books when he was a kid. So Parton wanted to make sure that books could be a part of every child's life.

Every month Dolly Parton's Imagination Library gave a free book to children up to the age of five. The program later expanded to five

countries, and almost two million children get a free book every month!

During the COVID-19 pandemic, Parton added a special feature to her Imagination Library: Goodnight with Dolly. Go to https://imaginationlibrary.com/goodnight-with-dolly-read-aloud/ to listen to this amazing hero read a bedtime story.

EXPLORE SOME MORE!

Are you a songwriter? Dolly Parton wrote her first song when she was five years old. You can write songs too! Parton wrote about what she knew, like her childhood. Try writing about your pet, your favorite food, or games you like to play. Visit https://www.kidzworld.com/article/24798-how-to-write-songs/ for tips about songwriting.

DIVE IN!

Dolly Parton: Diamond in a Rhinestone World by Leslie Holleran (Lerner Publications, 2023), 48 pages.

Dolly Parton's childhood cabin in the Great Smoky Mountains of Tennessee

WALTER PAYTON

SWEETNESS
FOOTBALL PLAYER
MAN OF THE YEAR
HUMANITARIAN

Everything you read about Walter Payton will mention what a nice guy he was. When he played football at Jackson State University in Mississippi, he earned the nickname Sweetness, and it stayed with him for the rest of his life. He was a friendly person who others loved to be around. The nickname also reflected his incredible moves on the field.

Was Payton's friendliness what made him a hero? Or was it his legendary football career with the Chicago Bears? For thirteen seasons in the National Football League (NFL), Payton set record after record with his running talents. He never gave up on a play. He was a fast and powerful runner with incredible moves who made defenders work really hard to stop him. Browse the internet to see videos of his spectacular plays with the Bears.

NFL fans agree that Payton was one of the greatest runners ever to play the game—many say he was *the* greatest. But what really made Sweetness a true hero was the way he played and his desire to give back to his community. He worked hard to be in the best physical shape for games, and he always played with sportsmanship and compassion for his opponents. When he wasn't playing the game he loved, he often helped people in his community. In 1977, in only his third year as a professional athlete, the NFL gave him their Man of the Year Award. The league recognized a player who

Walter Payton was the NFL MVP in 1977 and helped the Chicago Bears win the Super Bowl in 1986.

not only excelled on the football field but also shined as a humanitarian off the field.

Payton retired from the NFL when he was thirty-three. Tragically, he later developed cancer and died in 1999. To honor Sweetness, the NFL renamed the Man of the Year Award the Walter Payton Man of the Year Award. Players and fans continue to celebrate Payton's commitment to excellence on and off the field.

EXPLORE!
The Walter Payton Man of the Year Award is one of the greatest honors any professional athlete can win. Each of the thirty-two teams in the NFL nominates a player who showed excellence in playing the game of football and in helping

their communities—just as Walter Payton did. One player earns the award each season, but the thirty-two nominated players have already proven that they are winners to their hometown fans. Go to www.nfl.com /honors/man-of-the-year to see all the past winners and the most recent nominees. The winner is honored at the Super Bowl each season, the most watched sporting event in the US.

EXPLORE SOME MORE!

In 1988 Payton founded the Walter Payton Foundation to help children who lived in the

DIVE IN!

G.O.A.T. Football Running Backs by Alexander Lowe (Lerner Publications, 2023), 32 pages.

Never Die Easy: The Autobiography of Walter Payton by Walter Payton and Don Yaeger (Villard, 2000), 268 pages.

Chicago, Illinois, area. After Payton died in 1999, his wife, Connie, continued the work they had begun together. In 2001 the name changed to the Walter and Connie Payton Foundation (https://www.payton34.com).

One of the group's most important projects is encouraging people to sign up to be organ donors. Organ donors agree that when they die, doctors will remove important organs such as the liver, heart, and kidneys and give them to sick people who need them to survive. Had Walter Payton's illness been detected earlier, a liver transplant may have saved his life. The Walter and Connie Payton Foundation continues to promote organ donation and support programs that bring dignity and pride to the lives of children and US military veterans.

What are athletes in your community doing to help others? For example, athletes from Penn State University and other schools raise money for disease research by holding an annual weight-lifting event. Check it out at https:// www.upliftingathletes.org. What's happening near where you live?

POWER WORDS!

"Do anything that might make the world a better place for someone."

—*Walter Payton*

Walter Payton at the Pro Football Hall of Fame in Canton, Ohio, in July 1993

I. M. PEI

APRIL 26, 1917–MAY 16, 2019

MASTER BUILDER
ARCHITECT
DREAMER

Ieoh Ming (I. M.) Pei's father wanted him to become a doctor, but the sight of blood made him sick. He liked buildings. Maybe he could try architecture. He decided to study in the United States. He thought American movies were cool. Who knew that this teenager from Shanghai, China, would become I. M. Pei, the master builder?

His buildings have astonished millions of people around the world:

- The beautiful East Building of Washington, DC's National Gallery of Art
- The "glass pyramid" at the Louvre Museum in Paris (that's where the *Mona Lisa* is kept)
- The seventy-four-story Bank of China skyscraper in Hong Kong
- Even the Rock and Roll Hall of Fame and Museum in Cleveland, Ohio

Almost half of I. M. Pei's building designs have won major awards. In 1993 President George H. W. Bush awarded him the Presidential Medal of Freedom. Throughout his brilliant career, Pei lived up to his name, Ieoh Ming, which means "to inscribe brightly." What a smashing success story! All gain and no pain!

Well, almost. There *was* pain—*panes* actually. Like all people who achieve great things, I. M. Pei had his share of failures. The panes that caused him pain were in the John Hancock Tower in downtown Boston,

I. M. Pei smiles for the camera. In 1983 he won the Pritzker Architecture Prize for his significant achievement in the field.

Massachusetts. Built in the early 1970s, this tallest of Boston's skyscrapers was covered by pale blue sheets of glass. "Magnificent!" said the critics. The citizens of the city hailed this breathtaking structure . . . until the panes of glass started falling out!

But every problem has a solution *if* you don't give up. The panes were replaced with a more reliable type, and the pain of failure gave way to a renewed spirit of confidence. I. M. Pei had proven again what so many other heroes learned in their careers: never give up. No pain, no gain!

EXPLORE!
Among the honors that Pei has won is the Pritzker Architecture Prize. Some people call it

"Today, we rush everything, but architecture is slow, and the landscapes it sits in even slower." —*I. M. Pei*

the Nobel Prize of architecture. Pei used the $100,000 in prize money to set up a scholarship fund for Chinese students wanting to study architecture in the United States. The students then return to China to practice their profession. When they do, they can visit sites like Fragrant Hill, outside of Beijing. There, they'll see a hotel that Pei designed in the 1980s, nearly forty years after he left China. Although he had been in the United States since he was a teenager, Pei had remained tuned in to the relationship between nature and buildings that is important to the Chinese people. He designed Fragrant Hill with that relationship in mind, and it serves to inspire young architects in his homeland.

DIVE IN!

I.M. Pei: Architect of Time, Place, and Purpose by Jill Rubalcaba (Marshall Cavendish, 2011), 132 pages.

There's a major movement in the United States to make sure that great buildings are preserved. Children born even a hundred years from now should have an opportunity to see I. M. Pei's architectural wonders. Search the internet for these preservation efforts. Look for great buildings (such as the Empire State Building in New York), whole sections of cities (such as the colorful Art Deco section of Miami Beach), and off-the-wall roadside stuff (such as the very first McDonald's Golden Arches). Visit the National Trust for Historic Preservation website at https://savingplaces.org for more ideas. You might even get involved in saving the United States' great architecture for your grandchildren!

Although Pei's redesign of the entrance to the Louvre was initially controversial, the 66-foot-tall (20 m) glass-and-iron pyramid in the entryway has become synonymous with the Paris museum.

RONALD WILSON REAGAN

THE GREAT COMMUNICATOR
US PRESIDENT
GOVERNOR
ACTOR
AUTHOR

Before his political career, Ronald Reagan was a famous Hollywood actor. He appeared in dozens of films over three decades.

The Cold War may seem like ancient history to many people. But to Americans born before the early 1990s, the Cold War posed a threat for decades. The major players were the United States and the Soviet Union. Ronald Reagan's greatest achievement was helping to end this marathon struggle between the world's two superpowers.

Since the end of World War II, the United States and the Soviet Union were the world's biggest powers. The two nations were also bitter enemies, competing for resources and allies around the world. Both nations spent vast amounts of money on their militaries, and both developed incredibly powerful weapons of mass destruction that threatened all life on the planet. The United States and the Soviet Union didn't face each other directly on the battlefield—that's why it was called a cold war. But there was lots of tension, and from the 1950s through the 1980s, nuclear war was a very real and scary possibility.

President Reagan was determined to convince the Soviet Union that it could not win the Cold War. During his first term in office (1981–1985), he pursued peace by launching a massive buildup of the US military. Seems like a major contradiction, doesn't it? Why would

the president increase our military spending to bring peace? His objective was to show the Soviet Union that they could not match the military strength of the United States, and that it was pointless to try.

Reagan was a skillful negotiator and speaker. When new leadership arose in the Soviet Union, Reagan shifted his focus to diplomacy. He knew that if a nuclear war between the two superpowers ever did occur, there would be no winners—both countries would be destroyed. In the president's second term (1985–1989), he reached out to Mikhail Gorbachev, the Soviet leader. Gorbachev also wanted to reform the relationship between the United States and the

"Mr. Gorbachev, tear down this wall." —*Ronald Reagan*

Soviet Union. The leaders met several times over the next few years at what were known as summit meetings. They were able to come to historic agreements to reduce nuclear weapons stockpiles.

Reagan's skill as an orator rose to its highest level when he gave a speech on June 12, 1987, in Berlin, Germany. The Berlin Wall divided West Berlin from East Berlin, separating opposing sides in the Cold War. It was a major symbol of the conflict. Standing at the famous Brandenburg Gate, Reagan stated: "General Secretary Gorbachev, if you seek peace, if you seek prosperity for the Soviet Union and Eastern Europe, if you seek liberalization, come here to this gate! Mr. Gorbachev, open this gate! Mr. Gorbachev, tear down this wall!"

Reagan's dramatic words became real in November 1989 when the Berlin Wall was destroyed. Even though he was no longer president, Reagan saw one of his most cherished goals nearly achieved. The Cold War ended two years later when the Soviet Union collapsed.

EXPLORE!

Ronald Reagan was a popular president. Twice during his time in office his public job approval rating reached 68 percent. That meant more than two of every three Americans polled were pleased with his

DIVE IN!

Ronald Reagan: Our 40th President by Winston Groom (Regnery, 2012), 164 pages.

performance. One of the major reasons for his popularity was his skill as a speaker.

You can watch and listen to many of Reagan's speeches. Go to www.reaganfoundation.org, the official website of the Ronald Reagan Presidential Foundation and Institute. Click on "Ronald Reagan." Then scroll down to "Quotes and Speeches." You will find recordings of dozens of Reagan's speeches.

One of his many memorable speeches was given on January 28, 1986, when the space shuttle *Challenger* exploded after launching. Students in classrooms all across the United States and other people around the world were watching the launch live on TV and saw the terrible accident as the spacecraft burst into flames, killing all seven astronauts on board. That night Reagan went on national television to grieve with all Americans. As you watch and listen, you'll understand why so many people considered him an inspiring orator.

Ronald Reagan raises his hand to the crowd after his 1987 speech near the Brandenburg Gate in Berlin, Germany.

JACKIE ROBINSON AND BRANCH RICKEY

ROBINSON:
JANUARY 31, 1919–OCTOBER 24, 1972

RICKEY:
DECEMBER 20, 1881–DECEMBER 9, 1965

TEAM PLAYERS
BASEBALL CHAMPIONS
CIVIL RIGHTS TRAILBLAZERS

You probably can't conceive of an all-white Major League Baseball team. But in 1946—not that long ago—all of the sixteen major-league teams banned players, coaches, and team officials who were not white. It took a great player and a team executive who was ready for change to break baseball's racial barrier.

Go back to 1947. Baseball was *the* national pastime. At the time, there were two different baseball leagues. No, not the National League and American League. We're talking about the major leagues and the Negro leagues. Only white ballplayers could play in the majors and dream of making it to the World Series. Black players, no matter how good they were, played in their own league and were "kept in their place" as second-class athletes.

Then Branch Rickey came along. He was the president and general manager of the Brooklyn (now the Los Angeles) Dodgers, and he thought things had to be changed. He knew there were Black men who played ball as well as white men, and he knew they should be playing in the big leagues. But he also knew that segregation was a part of baseball and a part of the United States.

Jackie Robinson *(left)* and Branch Rickey posed for this photo on February 12, 1948, the day Robinson signed his contract to play another season for the Dodgers.

To integrate the game would not be easy.

Rickey determined that Jackie Roosevelt Robinson was the man who could survive the ordeal that integrating baseball would be. In late August 1945, shortly after the end of World War II, Rickey met with Robinson and asked him to join the Dodgers' farm team (the Montreal Royals) to prepare for the major leagues. Robinson was going to make history. This extraordinary meeting was one of the most dramatic episodes in sports. Many people believed in segregation and hated Black Americans. Rickey warned Robinson that if he decided to go through with this, he would be deliberately attacked. If he lost control, the people who opposed integration would pounce on his display of anger, no matter how justified, and push the whole effort back to square one.

POWER WORDS!

"A life is not important except in the impact it has on other lives." —*Jackie Robinson*

"I couldn't face God much longer knowing that his black creatures are held separate from his white creatures in the game that has given me all I own."

—*Branch Rickey (speaking to his grandson)*

At one point during their meeting, Robinson could no longer contain himself. He said, "Mr. Rickey, are you looking for a Negro who's afraid to fight back?"

With passion in his voice, Rickey replied, "I'm looking for a ballplayer, Jackie, with guts enough not to fight back."

Robinson joined the Royals, then the Dodgers, and Rickey was right. Fans, players, coaches, even some of his own teammates reacted with hate. But Robinson held on and played the game—the baseball game. And he played it very, very well.

The integration of our national pastime was a major step toward the integration of our society.

Both Robinson and Rickey went on to earn places in the Baseball Hall of Fame. And places in history as well.

DIVE IN!

Jackie Robinson: Athletes Who Made a Difference by Blake Hoena (Graphic Universe, 2020), 32 pages.

research. You might be surprised at how recently discrimination existed in some professional sports. For example, in 1997 Tiger Woods won the Masters Tournament, one of the biggest prizes in men's professional golf. Yet as late as 1974, no Black people had played in that major golf event. In fact, the "whites only" clause in the Professional Golfers' Association (PGA) was not erased until 1961.

Look around online and at your library, and see if you can identify heroic athletes of color who were the first to integrate your favorite sports. Let us in on their stories of courage and determination. Who knows?—maybe you'll uncover a hero for our next list of 60!

EXPLORE!

Jackie Robinson and Branch Rickey integrated baseball, but how about other sports? Did white and Black people always play on the same football and basketball teams? How about sports such as swimming, tennis, and ice-skating? Pick a sport (or several) and do a little

Jackie Robinson (*left*) poses in his Dodgers uniform before his team played the New York Giants in 1949. All four players pictured here were selected for that year's All-Star team.

FRED ROGERS

MISTER ROGERS
TELEVISION HOST
AUTHOR
MINISTER

Fred Rogers wanted *everyone* to be his neighbor. For thirty-three years, he welcomed TV viewers to the marvelous, magical *Mister Rogers' Neighborhood*.

There was nothing really fancy about the show. It didn't have high-tech gimmicks and special effects. The cast included Fred Rogers and his human and puppet friends.

What exactly did happen on *Mister Rogers' Neighborhood*? Just about everything. He wanted kids to learn about the real world. He invited his neighbors to explore fun things like making crayons and learning to dance. He talked about sad things, like the end of a marriage or a dying pet, in ways that kids could understand. Sometimes well-known guests stopped by the neighborhood. Yo-Yo Ma (see page 76) visited the show and played his cello.

Most of the time, Rogers taught kids about everyday life. He answered questions such as what happens at a bakery, how is your mail delivered, and where does milk come from?

In every visit to *Mister Rogers' Neighborhood*, viewers learned about positive feelings and actions like imagination, kindness, respect, and acceptance. Although the show was meant for young children, everyone was welcome. You can watch episodes of *Mister Rogers' Neighborhood* online. Maybe someday *you* will share a visit to the neighborhood with people who are special to you.

Fred Rogers on the set of his show, *Mister Rogers' Neighborhood*. The show aired from 1968 to 2001.

POWER WORDS!

"Look for the helpers. You will always find people who are helping." —*Fred Rogers*

EXPLORE!

One of the best things about visiting *Mister Rogers' Neighborhood* was knowing that you would be welcome. It didn't matter what you looked like, what your parents did to earn

Rogers (*right*) laughs with Mr. McFeely, one of *Mister Rogers' Neighborhood*'s many recurring characters, during a rehearsal for the show in 1993.

money, or if you lived in a big house or a small house. The only thing that mattered was treating other people with kindness.

Rogers had a different experience when he was a child. His classmates bullied him! They called him names because of his weight and because he was shy. In high school, he began to make good friends, the bullying stopped, and Rogers began to shine. Bullying happens way too often, but there are people and programs trying to prevent it. Visit https://www.pacer.org/bullying/ for a lot of great anti-bullying strategies.

DIVE IN!

Kindness and Wonder: Why Mister Rogers Matters Now More Than Ever by Gavin Edwards (Dey Street, 2019), 248 pages.

Who Was Mister Rogers? by Diane Bailey (Penguin Workshop, 2019), 107 pages.

EXPLORE SOME MORE!

Have you ever heard of 143 Day? It's a day of kindness inspired by Fred Rogers. He used 143 as a special code for "I love you." To crack the code, think about the letters in the sentence. *I* has one letter, *love* has four letters, and *you* has three letters. In Pennsylvania, 143 Day is celebrated on May 23, the 143rd day of the year. Pennsylvanians perform acts of kindness on that day in honor of Rogers. Some people would like to see 143 Day go national! Google it and see if you would like to get your community involved.

ELEANOR ROOSEVELT

OCTOBER 11, 1884–NOVEMBER 7, 1962

"FIRST LADY OF THE WORLD"

HUMANITARIAN
DIPLOMAT
FIRST LADY
AUTHOR

*L*onely, sad, afraid—**these words barely begin to describe Eleanor as a child.** But this shy little girl couldn't stay frightened forever. Not when others were feeling excluded and unwanted too.

The United States in the 1930s was a racially divided land. Many white citizens blindly carried on their parents' and grandparents' prejudices against people of color. But not Eleanor Roosevelt. She was the wife of a popular president, Franklin Delano Roosevelt (FDR), who led our country through the Great Depression and most of World War II. Eleanor believed with all her heart the words of our Declaration of Independence: that all people are created equal and have equal rights—life, liberty, and the pursuit of happiness. And while being afraid was part of her childhood, Eleanor wasn't afraid as an adult to stand up for her beliefs.

For example, in 1939 Black singer Marian Anderson was to perform at Constitution Hall in Washington, DC. She was an incredibly gifted opera singer. But some of the members of the Daughters of the American Revolution (DAR) objected to a Black person singing in their auditorium and canceled the performance. Eleanor, a lifelong member of the DAR, was outraged. She immediately quit the group, then

Eleanor Roosevelt was the wife of a president, but she is best remembered as a hands-on social activist.

helped arrange a new location for the concert. On Easter Sunday, Marian Anderson proudly sang in front of the Lincoln Memorial, and seventy-five thousand people came to listen.

During that same year, Eleanor attended a meeting in Birmingham, Alabama, where state law forbade white and Black people from sitting together in public places. Well, she simply refused to obey the law and sit on the "white side" of the meeting room. Instead, she had a chair placed in the room's center aisle. There she sat, showing the Alabama legislators what she thought of their segregation laws.

Eleanor's life reflected her commitment to public service in our country and throughout the world. As FDR's wife, she energized and transformed the role of First Lady. Later, as his widow, she served as a delegate to the United Nations and kept on with her humanitarian work: always fighting racial injustice, working tirelessly for social reform—and earning the title "First Lady of the World."

At the time of her death, the shy, lonely, scared little girl was the most recognized individual in the world.

EXPLORE!

While our Constitution doesn't even mention the role of a president's spouse, we are always interested in the chief executive's family. The First Lady, in particular, can draw a lot of attention to a special cause. Eleanor Roosevelt

DIVE IN!

Eleanor Roosevelt, Fighter for Justice: Her Impact on the Civil Rights Movement, the White House, and the World by Ilene Cooper (Abrams, 2018), 192 pages.

transformed the role of First Lady by using her position to embrace the world. Have others followed in her footsteps? Use your library or the internet to research First Ladies since Eleanor Roosevelt's time. What were their interests and concerns? How did they draw attention to important issues of the day, such as literacy, the war on drugs, historic preservation, and the beautification of the United States?

What do you think the president's spouse should work on? As you read about the 60 amazing people in this book, a particular idea or cause connected with one of these heroes may catch your attention. Should the First Lady promote Roberto Clemente's program for young athletes? Or support Alex's Lemonade Stand Foundation by setting up a lemonade stand at the White House? Find out more about the current president's spouse at https://www .whitehouse.gov/administration/.

POWER WORDS!

"No one can make you feel inferior without your consent."

—*Eleanor Roosevelt*

Eleanor Roosevelt (left) appears with singer Marian Anderson at a ceremony honoring Anderson on July 2, 1939. Roosevelt was a longtime supporter of Anderson and fought against discriminatory laws.

FRANKLIN D. ROOSEVELT

JANUARY 30, 1882–APRIL 12, 1945

MR. PRESIDENT
US PRESIDENT
AUTHOR

Franklin D. Roosevelt was elected president of the United States four times and led our nation through the Great Depression and most of World War II. Roosevelt spent the last twenty-four years of his life in a wheelchair because of polio. Usually this disease affected children, which is why it was also called infantile paralysis. It struck Franklin when he was thirty-nine years old, a father of five children and well into his national political career. This illness changed FDR's life forever. The man who had loved to hike, play tennis, and sail now depended on other people to dress and undress him.

It was more than a physical challenge he faced. He had to deal with the mental challenge too. Franklin had lived a life of luxury and privilege.

As a privileged young man at Groton, a private school, Franklin had been influenced by his caring headmaster (principal) the Reverend Endicott Peabody. Peabody wanted the wealthy boys to provide leadership and public service for others not as fortunate.

Now privileged Franklin felt helpless. Now he could truly understand what his headmaster had meant. When he became president, the Great Depression had left one-third of all Americans hungry and homeless. He vowed to help these unfortunate people in any way he

Franklin D. Roosevelt was well known for his frequent fireside chats, which were informal radio talks. It was his way of explaining his programs directly to the American people and thus eliciting their support.

could. FDR's leadership and his charisma (his personal magnetism) led our country through some of its most troubled times.

EXPLORE!

Here's an opportunity for you to become an oral historian, someone who learns about the past by talking to people who lived it. You find out what they know about people and events of long ago by asking them good questions. After you read more about FDR, try it.

Your grandparents or great-grandparents, your older uncles and aunts, elderly neighbors and friends, may have been alive when FDR

"So first of all let me assert my firm belief that the only thing we have to fear is fear itself."

—Franklin D. Roosevelt

was our president. Those people are now in their eighties and nineties. We should capture their stories while these witnesses to history are still alive. Ask them how they felt about him. Did they listen to his fireside chats on their radios? Did they like how he led the country? Did they cry when they heard the news that he had died? Ask if they knew that FDR used a wheelchair. Are you surprised by that question? Well, most Americans in the 1930s and 1940s did *not* know this about their president. That's because newspaper photographers and filmmakers agreed not to show him in a wheelchair. The press was free to do so, but they didn't. Why do you think they made that decision?

DIVE IN!

Franklin D. Roosevelt by Melissa Maupin (Child's World, 2020), 48 pages.

Record your interviews. Of course, you can take notes of your conversation, but you have to be very careful to make sure you write down exactly what the person is telling you.

Visit www.heroes4us.com to send us your oral history of FDR so we can learn from you.

EXPLORE SOME MORE!

Bring this gigantic historical figure alive for yourself. Visit in person or online the places that were important to Franklin D. Roosevelt and his wife, Eleanor Roosevelt (see page 100):

- Franklin D. Roosevelt Presidential Library and Museum, www.fdrlibrary.org
- Home of Franklin D. Roosevelt, www.nps.gov/hofr
- Roosevelt Campobello International Park, www.nps.gov/roca
- Roosevelt's Little White House, www.nps.gov/nr/travel/presidents /roosevelts_little_white_house.html

Also check out the Franklin Delano Roosevelt Memorial at www.nps.gov/frde. This impressive memorial was dedicated in 1997 in Washington, DC.

Franklin D. Roosevelt *(center)* **walks with help in 1933. Polio had made his legs weak and unable to support him on their own.**

THEODORE ROOSEVELT

OCTOBER 27, 1858–JANUARY 6, 1919

THE CONSERVATION PRESIDENT
**US PRESIDENT
CONSERVATIONIST
ADVENTURER
NOBEL PEACE PRIZE WINNER
AUTHOR**

A portrait of Theodore Roosevelt taken in 1911

In the late 1800s and the early part of the twentieth century, the Industrial Age changed the United States. More people came to the United States and built cities and towns. Teddy Roosevelt realized that all this progress could devour the US wilderness if we weren't careful. A good friend of his named John Muir (see page 80) talked to Roosevelt about the need to preserve our national wilderness. Teddy Roosevelt became the first US president to take major action to protect the environment.

During his seven and a half years in the White House, Roosevelt designated 150 national forests; fifty-five bird and game preserves; five national parks (including Yosemite); and eighteen national monuments, such as the Grand Canyon. Though an avid hunter, he once said: "More and more, as it becomes necessary to preserve the game, let us hope that the camera will largely supplant the rifle." More than sixty years later, in honor of Teddy Roosevelt's devotion to preserving the natural United States, the National Wildlife Federation awarded him first place in its Conservation Hall of Fame.

But Teddy Roosevelt wasn't only a giant in the world of conservation. He was also a dynamo in a hundred other ways. Before he became president, Roosevelt was colonel of the Rough Riders during the Spanish-American War (1898), governor of New York, a police commissioner, and a sheriff. Did you know he was also a founder of the Intercollegiate Athletic Association, which is now the National Collegiate Athletic Association (NCAA)? He ran a ranch out west, traveled all over the world, and raised six kids. He also managed to write thirty-five books and more than *150,000* letters to tons of people.

He did lots more after moving into the White House. He even won the Nobel Peace Prize. Not bad for someone who was frequently ill as a child

"It is not what we have that will make us a great nation. It is the way in which we use it." —*Theodore Roosevelt*

and had been schooled for many years at home because of his frail health.

EXPLORE!

Across the country, areas large and small are being transformed from pavement to parkland. People are seeing the value of open space, even in the middle of congested cities. Is anything like this happening in your community? Maybe a neighborhood association is cleaning trash from a vacant lot and "greening it up." Your school, library, or newspaper might have information about local reclamation activities. Is anyone protesting the project? Who and why? Do you agree with them?

If you think the project is worthwhile, see if you can help. If work is just beginning, offer to take photographs of the site before, during, and after the cleanup is done. Share your photos online and they could become part of your community's archives—part of history.

From the time he was a boy, Teddy Roosevelt understood that bringing nature to people would help them appreciate it. In his room, he set up his very own natural history "museum," displaying specimens of insects, birds, and animals he had collected. He charged adults a one-penny admission, while kids could view it for free if they helped out by feeding his critters.

DIVE IN!

Theodore Roosevelt's Presidency by Heather E. Schwartz (Lerner Publications, 2017), 104 pages

Teddy's museum may have helped some of those kids look at nature in a whole new way. The pictures you take in your community can make a difference too. They may encourage future generations to preserve your local "green space" by showing how ugly it became when it was neglected.

EXPLORE SOME MORE!

To learn even more about this amazing hero, visit www.theodoreroosevelt.org.

Like Roosevelt himself, the first family was young, energetic, and a novelty in the White House. Public interest in them was spontaneous, as pictures of Theodore, Edith, and their six children began appearing in newspapers and magazines. For once in history, the executive mansion acquired aspects of a normal American home, complete with roller skates, bicycles, and tennis rackets.

JONAS SALK

OCTOBER 28, 1914–JUNE 23, 1995

MEDICAL PIONEER
PHYSICIAN
RESEARCHER
HUMANITARIAN
AUTHOR

Believe in what you do. Dr. Jonas Salk did. In fact, he believed so strongly in the quality of his medical research that he was willing to risk his own safety to prove that he was right. His wife and his three sons put their lives and health on the line for him too. A researcher doesn't usually test his own findings, especially on himself and his family. But Dr. Jonas Salk did.

Polio, the short name for poliomyelitis, was a dreaded childhood disease. Most people with polio contracted the disease in infancy, which is why it was also known as infantile paralysis. Could a cure be found to stop this disease? Did people believe they would ever be free from the danger of polio? Dr. Jonas Salk did.

He worked sixteen hours a day, seven days a week for years to find a way to prevent the disease from affecting kids. Finally, he created a vaccine to immunize people against polio. After successful tests on laboratory animals, it had to be tested on human beings. Who would take the risk? Dr. Jonas Salk did.

Why did the tests involve risks? Because the vaccine consisted of the actual poliovirus. That's right, to prevent the disease from occurring, the disease was actually injected into your body. Pretty scary thought. The killed poliovirus cells in the vaccine built up natural antibodies (fighting cells) in the body. Did people believe the new vaccine would work? Dr. Jonas Salk did.

Jonas Salk devoted his life to finding a vaccine for polio. Here he appears in his lab at the University of Pittsburgh on October 7, 1954.

POWER WORDS!

"The reward for work well done is the opportunity to do more." —*Dr. Jonas Salk*

Because they trusted him, Dr. Salk's wife and children also volunteered to be "human guinea pigs." The tests were successful in that they showed the vaccine was not dangerous: none of the people injected with the vaccine got polio. This allowed the vaccine to be tested on a larger scale, eventually proving itself to prevent polio.

It was *the* major breakthrough in the 1950s and was the beginning of the end of polio's terrible effects. It was clear to everyone what Jonas Salk had done.

A grateful nation and world applauded his achievement. He could have become a very wealthy man from his discovery, but when asked who would control the polio vaccine, he replied, "There is no patent. Could you patent the sun?" No, such beneficial work should be freely shared—and that's what Dr. Jonas Salk had done. Dr. Salk GAVE his discovery away so the vaccine could be available to everyone who needed it—that's a true hero!

EXPLORE!

The legacy of Dr. Salk's medical research continues at the Salk Institute for Biological Studies. To find out what its latest research

DIVE IN!
The War against Polio
by Cynthia O'Brien
(Crabtree, 2022),
32 pages.

efforts are, check it out online at www.salk.edu. You can find out about the institute's research on COVID-19, AIDS, Alzheimer's disease, birth defects, the brain, cancer, gene therapy, hormones, multiple sclerosis, and more.

Dr. Salk himself, even at the age of eighty, was actively involved in research to find a cure for AIDS or a vaccine to prevent its spread. What do you know about AIDS? What do you know about other infectious diseases, such as the flu, pneumonia, or even the common cold? As an American, you have access to incredible medical services. Some people say that we have the best doctors and health-care facilities in the world. The cost of all these services has become very high. You can be part of an effort to keep our health system top rate by learning ways to stay healthy. Do you know the right kinds of foods to eat? Do you know the importance of daily exercise? Do you know how you can reduce the chance of getting a disease such as AIDS?

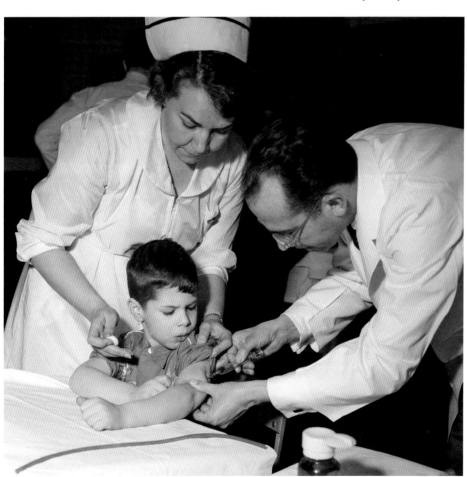

Dr. Salk administers a shot of polio vaccine to a young patient. His breakthrough made him a national hero, and he was honored at the White House by President Dwight D. Eisenhower.

ALEXANDRA (ALEX) SCOTT

Alex Scott always maintained a positive outlook. In her memory, Alex's Lemonade Stand Foundation is dedicated to finding cures for all forms of childhood cancer.

JANUARY 18, 1996–AUGUST 1, 2004

GOOD SAMARITAN
MIRACLE WORKER
DREAMER

How much would you pay for a glass of lemonade? Fifty cents? One dollar? If you knew that by buying a lemonade you could help sick children, would you pay even more? Lots of people—millions of people in the United States and other countries—have paid more than one dollar for their cup of lemonade. And they're happy they did. They have been inspired to buy lemonade by a little girl named Alex.

Just a short time before Alex's first birthday, doctors told her parents their daughter had a disease called neuroblastoma, a cancer that causes nerve cells to grow out of control. Neuroblastoma usually affects only young children. It is a deadly disease, but there are several treatments that can improve and prolong a patient's life. Doctors told her family that even if she could beat the disease, she would probably never be able to walk.

Alex began treatments immediately, and the young girl fought courageously to stay strong over the next few years. At the age of four, she made a decision that would ultimately change tens of thousands of lives. Alex decided she wanted to set up a lemonade stand in her front yard and give the money she earned to her hospital to fight cancer. With the help of her family she did just that, and together they raised $2,000 to help fight pediatric cancer.

The next year, Alex and her family relocated from Connecticut to Pennsylvania. She was treated at the world-famous Children's Hospital of Philadelphia and continued to raise money for cancer research. But even with the most modern medical care, her disease couldn't be stopped. Alex died at the age of eight.

EXPLORE!
Did you think that Alex's story ended when she died? Her death was actually just the end of a chapter. The tale of Alex and her lemonade stand

POWER WORDS!

"I'm Alex, I'm eight years old. I have neuroblastoma and I raise money for pediatric cancer research with the help of other kids and grown-ups through my lemonade stand. I give the money I raise to research to find cures for pediatric cancers." —*Alex Scott*

continues. The courage and the caring Alex demonstrated in her life has led to lemonade stands popping up in communities all around the country. Those neighborhood lemonade sellers, along with generous individual and corporate donors, have raised over $200 million. The money has funded hundreds of research projects to help find a cure for cancer in children. Not only is lemonade better for your health than soda pop, it's better for the health of all children fighting cancer!

How can you help? You guessed it—set up a lemonade stand! Go to www.alexslemonade.org for instructions. Alex's whole family is there to help you. Her mom and dad (Liz and Jay) and her brothers (Patrick, Eddie, and Joey) all help raise money to battle cancer, just as Alex did.

Looking for other ways to help? Visit https://www.alexslemonade.org/campaign/kids-corner for some ideas. For example, you can ask guests at your birthday party to donate to Alex's Lemonade Stand Foundation instead of giving you presents. Or maybe raising money through a walkathon is more your speed. There are lots of ways to pitch in to fight cancer!

EXPLORE SOME MORE!

Many charitable organizations and hospitals around the world fight childhood cancer. Why not find out more about them and how to help fight the disease? A great example is St. Jude

DIVE IN!

Alexandra Scott by Gail B. Stewart (KidHaven, 2006), 64 pages.

Children's Research Hospital in Memphis, Tennessee. Visit its website at www.stjude.org to learn more about cancer treatment and research.

Alex was a Good Samaritan, and you can be one too. Not sure what a Good Samaritan is? Google it!

Alex Scott enjoyed selling lemonade, but she liked helping people even more. Here she is at one of her lemonade stands.

TECUMSEH

SHOOTING STAR
STATESMAN
WARRIOR

If you have studied our country's history carefully, you know that before our Constitution was adopted in 1788, we were governed by a document called the Articles of Confederation.

Confederation means "a joining together for a common purpose." The newly independent American colonies joined together as states in a confederation. Their unity gave them strength.

That's exactly what Tecumseh tried to do with numerous Native American tribes. White people were sweeping across the country, taking land from Native nations and offering little or no compensation. Tecumseh worked hard to unite a number of nations into a strong Shawnee Confederation that could resist this invasion. But it wasn't easy. The members of each tribe were fiercely proud of their individual tribal identities and leaderships.

Tecumseh was a gifted speaker. His words convinced Native Americans that unity would help them hold on to their land. Traveling thousands of miles through the territory east of the Mississippi River, Tecumseh forged the largest united group of Native nations ever. In 1808 he and his brother, Tenskwatawa, called the Prophet, established a village called Prophetstown. There, confederation members could follow traditional Native American ways and train to defend their land.

Despite its unity, however, the confederation was still unable to halt the westward movement

A reproduction of a portrait of Tecumseh from around 1790. The original watercolor painting was created by Mathais Noheimer.

of white settlers. In 1811 Tecumseh's brother sent the unified warriors into battle against white soldiers, although Tecumseh warned that the confederation was not yet strong enough. The warriors were defeated. Prophetstown was destroyed. The Native Americans were scattered.

Like the shooting star that streaked across the sky the night Tecumseh was born, the Shawnee Confederation shone brightly, brilliantly, for a moment. Then it was gone. But just as the image of that shooting star loomed large in the memories of those who saw it, Tecumseh's legacy as a man of influence lives on. Respect for him extends far beyond the Native American community. Throughout our country, you will find towns, schools, even a navy submarine named in his honor.

"Sell a country! Why not sell the air, the clouds, and the great sea as well as the earth? Did not the Great Spirit make them all for the use of his children?" —*Tecumseh*

EXPLORE!

Too much of our history was a violent struggle for the control of land—between the Native nations and those who came to this continent from other areas of the world. In most cases, compromises were rejected, and the solution was an "all or nothing" one. Usually, the Native Americans were the losers.

Tecumseh's story of loyalty to his people and devotion to his land is only one of countless Native American efforts to hold on to their heritage. As a country, we have finally honored the cultures and contributions of Native Americans. Opened in 2004, the National Museum of the American Indian is located on the famous Mall in our nation's capital. There, great Native American leaders such as

DIVE IN!

Tecumseh: Shooting Star of the Shawnee by Dwight Jon Zimmerman (Sterling, 2010), 124 pages.

Tecumseh: Speech at Vincennes by Rebecca Sjonger (Crabtree, 2019), 48 pages.

Tecumseh, Chief Joseph, Crazy Horse, Sitting Bull, and so many others have their stories told. Cultural artifacts from the Cherokee, Shawnee, Sioux, Hopi, and many other tribes and nations are displayed. Visitors can see and participate in ceremonies, performances, and educational activities celebrating Native American heritage. Visit the museum online at https://americanindian.si.edu.

EXPLORE SOME MORE!

In a growing number of areas around our country, Native American festivals are being held. Some of these are called powwows. Maybe you have attended some of these events yourself. If not, talk to your family or friends about going to a festival. Explore your local history resources (museums, websites, and local historians) to learn more about Native nations in your area and around the United States.

Tecumseh is shown here with General William Henry Harrison, who would later become the ninth president of the United States. Harrison badly defeated the unified Native American groups led by Tecumseh and his brother at the Battle of Tippecanoe.

HARRY S. TRUMAN

"GIVE 'EM HELL, HARRY"
US PRESIDENT
AUTHOR

"The buck stops here."

"Always do right. This will gratify some people and astonish the rest." (Mark Twain)

"If you can't stand the heat, get out of the kitchen."

These are three of Harry Truman's **favorite sayings.** In fact, the first two were printed on placards that he kept on his desk. And they weren't just empty slogans. These words guided Truman as he made tough decisions for our country during and after World War II, the most devastating global war in the history of the human race.

During that war, the United States, the guardian of democracy, had separate army companies for Black soldiers and white soldiers. That's right. Black people who served in either the army or navy were kept apart from white soldiers and sailors. Though they loyally defended the United States against Nazi Germany and imperial Japan in World War II, Black servicepeople were treated as second-class citizens in the country for which they had risked their lives.

Harry Truman knew it was wrong to segregate Black people from white people in the military. So, too, did previous presidents, but they chose not to deal with the problem. Not Harry Truman. It was wrong, and he had to change it. The Declaration of Independence said that all people are created equal and should have equal rights. It was that simple.

Every poll predicted that Republican presidential candidate Thomas Dewey would win a landslide victory in the election of 1948, and some newspapers actually reported Dewey's victory. But through hard campaigning, Harry Truman pulled off one of the biggest upsets in US political history.

POWER WORDS!

"The Bill of Rights applies to everybody in this country, and don't you ever forget it." —*Harry S. Truman*

End of discussion. So in 1948, Harry Truman issued an executive order integrating the US Armed Services.

Think of what that meant. Black and white sailors would be in the same units on ships, serving together. Black and white soldiers would march side by side. Black US pilots would train with white US pilots.

Nearly every admiral and general, as well as his civilian advisers on military matters, tried to talk Truman out of this. But he was the president, the commander in chief. He knew it was the right thing to do ("Always do right."). He made the tough decisions (the "buck" stopped with him). He wasn't afraid of the heat.

Some historians say that Harry Truman made more tough decisions than any other modern president did. Some of the decisions didn't solve the problems, but most of them did. And no one, friend or foe, can ever accuse him of not doing his job.

EXPLORE!

Harry S. Truman was guided by the slogans he kept on his desk. Every day they reminded him of how he wanted to conduct himself. "The buck stops here" meant he accepted responsibility. Do you? When you make a

DIVE IN!

Harry S. Truman by Robert Dallek (Times Books, 2008), 183 pages.

mistake, do you own up to it or do you try to "pass the buck"?

Find at least two slogans from famous quotes that can help you become a more responsible individual. Where do you look? Use the internet to find quotes that appeal to your desire to be a better person. Read lots of them before you make your selections. And don't forget to read the Power Words in this book!

Harry Truman had his slogans right in front of him, so you do the same. Put the quotes you've chosen on your computer's desktop. Design a poster of your quotes for your room. Place the quotes on your mirror. Share them with your family by placing them on the refrigerator. Hang some in your room. And just like Truman, put Mark Twain's words about always doing right in a prominent spot too.

EXPLORE SOME MORE!

Visit the Harry S. Truman National Historic Site at www.nps.gov/hstr and the Harry S. Truman Library & Museum at www.trumanlibrary.gov to explore the life and career of this great man. Don't miss the cool activity ideas at www.trumanlibrary.gov /education/student -resources/activity-sheets.

Harry Truman seated at his desk

HARRIET TUBMAN

CA. 1819 OR 1820–MARCH 10, 1913

MOSES
ABOLITIONIST
FREEDOM FIGHTER

This portrait of Harriet Tubman is from the 1860s.

The Promised Land. In Bible stories, it's the place of safety and freedom where the people of Israel were headed, led by a man named Moses. In the 1800s, the people seeking safety and freedom were enslaved Americans. The "Promised Land" was the northern part of our country, where slavery was against the law. And Harriet Tubman was "Moses." And if Harriet Tubman were leading you from slavery to freedom, you'd better not change your mind.

Escaping from slavery was incredibly dangerous for both the escapees and for those helping them escape. Enslaved people were considered the property of their owners. Helping an enslaved person run away was like stealing. People who ran away and were recaptured were in big trouble. Enslavers would haul them back, beat them, and make their lives even more miserable than before. Harriet Tubman managed to escape from slavery, but she didn't settle into a quiet life of freedom. Instead, she kept going back to lead others to the Promised Land. About seventy others, altogether. She led them through fields and woods to a series of safe houses, where people lived who would help enslaved people find freedom. This network of hiding places wasn't a train, but it was called the Underground Railroad. Harriet was one of the Railroad's courageous "conductors."

Once someone decided to hop on the Railroad, there was no turning back. Harriet Tubman made sure of that. When somebody got too scared to go on, Harriet would sometimes "encourage" the person by pointing a gun at their head! She knew that going to the Promised Land was risky. But going back to slavery was worse.

Angry slaveholders hated Harriet. They offered a huge reward for her capture. Everyone was looking for her. But this conductor of the Underground Railroad was never caught. And neither was any enslaved person she led to freedom.

EXPLORE!

Thousands of enslaved people seeking freedom owed their lives and their liberty to the Underground Railroad. The huge network of safe places leading to freedom was maintained

"On my Underground Railroad, I never ran my train off the track, and I never lost a passenger."

—*Harriet Tubman*

Harriet Tubman *(far left)*, **who once sought her own freedom from slavery, returned to the South nineteen times and helped about seventy people escape to freedom. She is shown here with some of the people she helped lead out of slavery.**

by hundreds of brave people who saw slavery for what it was: a vicious evil that had to be abolished.

Lots of books and articles have been written about the Underground Railroad, but there's been no way of tracing all the routes and identifying the Railroad "stations" as they are today. But all that is changing. The US National Park Service has conducted a study to figure out the best way to preserve and remember the Underground Railroad. The sheer size of the Railroad makes this an awesome task. We're talking about thousands of miles of roads and paths through almost three dozen states and parts of Canada. There were also hundreds of safe houses, and some of them are gone now.

Find out more about this

gigantic project by exploring the National Park Service website at www.nps.gov/nr/travel /underground. Find out if the Underground Railroad passed through your community. If it did, maybe you can get involved in the preservation effort.

EXPLORE SOME MORE!

In 2004 a museum opened in Cincinnati called the National Underground Railroad Freedom Center. The site on the Ohio River was chosen because it was "at the crossroads of freedom's journey" on the Underground Railroad. The museum was designed to promote understanding, healing, and reconciliation. Check it out at www.freedomcenter.org.

DIVE IN!

Harriet Tubman: Abolitionist and American Hero, by Niki Ahrens (Lerner Publications, 2022), 32 pages.

Harriet Tubman: Toward Freedom by Kazimir Lee and Whit Taylor (Little, Brown and Company, 2021), 99 pages.

MADAM C. J. WALKER

ONE IN A MILLION
BUSINESSPERSON
PHILANTHROPIST
ACTIVIST

She did it! Madam C. J. Walker was one of the first Black women to become a self-made millionaire. That means she earned her money. She didn't inherit it from her family or win some big prize. She worked hard for her money, and then she worked hard at giving it away.

The prices for products and services usually rise over long periods, causing the value of money to fall. A million dollars is still a lot of money, but it was an amazing total in 1900. Walker was one of about five thousand US millionaires that year, and one of the few women. More than ten million millionaires currently live in the US!

Just how did Walker earn that much money? She succeeded because she had a sharp business sense and the will to work tirelessly. Walker developed skin- and hair-care products for Black women. The products she developed were very popular. At the height of her success, thousands of women worked for her. They went door-to-door, selling products and teaching people how to use them.

As her wealth grew, so too did her fame and generosity. Walker worked to improve the lives of Black people. She gave money to many Black institutions, including the Florida school run by Mary McLeod Bethune (see p. 16). Walker died in 1919 at the age of fifty-one. In her will, she

This portrait of Madam C. J. Walker hangs in the National Portrait Gallery in Washington, DC.

ordered that more than half of all future profits of the Madame C. J. Walker Company go to charity. Had she not died so young, who knows how much more she might have accomplished?

EXPLORE!
The website www.madamcjwalker.com is packed with interesting information about Madam C. J. Walker's life and self-made success. As you click around the website, you'll see that her family played a huge role in her journey as a businessperson. Her great-great granddaughter, A'Lelia Bundles, still carries on the family's

Madam C. J. Walker's Wonderful Hair Grower was one of her company's best-selling products.

DIVE IN!

All about Madam C.J. Walker by A'Lelia Bundles (Blue River, 2017), 128 pages.

legacy. The 2020 TV miniseries *Self Made: Inspired by the Life of Madam C. J. Walker* is based on a book that Bundles wrote (see the DIVE IN! section on this page). Bundles has done a great job of gathering videos, photos, and articles that bring to life the story of her amazing great-great grandmother. Visit Bundles's website at https://aleliabundles.com/.

POWER WORDS!

"Don't sit down and wait for the opportunities to come. Get up and make them." —*Madam C. J. Walker*

EXPLORE SOME MORE!

Madam C. J. Walker developed hair-care products and cosmetics for Black women because not many similar products existed then. Can you think of a product or service that would help *your* community? Put on your imagination cap, and think of an idea for a business that would help people.

To get your creativity flowing, read about Mikaila Ulmer at https://www.meandthebees .com/. Mikaila sells lemonade and other items and donates some of the money she earns to protect bees and their habitats. Bonus fact: Alexandra Scott (see page 110), one of the heroes in this book, also sold lemonade and started a movement that is having an impact all over the US.

GEORGE WASHINGTON

FEBRUARY 22, 1732–DECEMBER 14, 1799

FATHER OF OUR COUNTRY
US PRESIDENT
COMMANDER IN CHIEF

Every country in the 1700s had kings or queens or emperors. George Washington was a loyal subject of the king of Great Britain. He was proud to be British and eager to serve his king and country. He had risked his life defending British rule in the colonies in the French and Indian War (1754–1763). But the king and his advisers mistreated the American colonies until the colonists finally said "Enough!" The Revolutionary War followed, and in 1776 the United States of America became an independent nation. George Washington led America's troops to victory over the British.

During the war for independence, a group of officers pleaded with Washington to declare himself "king." But the general told them that they were fighting for freedom and a new form of self-government. It made no sense to trade one King George (III) for a new King George! After the war, he retired as a true war hero to his Mount Vernon, Virginia, plantation. There he watched the new nation take shape.

With the acceptance of the Constitution in 1788, all eyes turned to the general to lead the new government. Would he accept the newly created office of "president"? He really wanted to stay at home. He was not seeking political power.

But George Washington was a humble man of strong character and solid virtues—and he believed in democracy. He agreed to be president because he believed that people should choose their leaders, and the people wanted him.

George Washington is one of the most recognizable figures in United States history. No photos of Washington exist, but numerous portraits give us a good idea of what the first president looked like.

DIVE IN!

George Washington's Presidency by Krystyna Poray Goddu (Lerner Publications, 2016), 104 pages.

Washington at Valley Forge by Russell Freedman (Holiday House, 2020), 100 pages.

President Washington's leadership and personal charisma shaped our young country as no other person could have done. He was indeed, "first in war, first in peace, and first in the hearts of his countrymen." (Richard Henry Lee, a good friend and fellow soldier, said that about Washington.)

EXPLORE!

To honor the Father of Our Country, we have used his name in many different places. We wonder how humble George would react to all this fuss! First, there's Washington, DC, capital of our nation and possibly the most important city in the world. What a wonderful place to visit. And what a great tribute to the great man who helped plan the Federal City but never lived there.

How many other places in this country are named for George Washington? Use the internet to find out. You'll be amazed! Do any other famous Americans have as many places named after them? If not, who ranks second and third after Washington?

Another great tribute to our first president is the world-famous Washington Monument. Did you know that no building in the capital city may be taller than the Washington Monument? Why? This 555-foot (169 m) obelisk has a fascinating history. Find out all about it at www.nps.gov/wamo.

And did you know that there's actually a second tower in Washington's honor only 5 miles (8 km) from the famous one? You'll find information on the "other Washington Monument" at www.gwmemorial.org.

EXPLORE SOME MORE!

Take a virtual tour of George Washington's Mount Vernon home at https://www.mountvernon.org. You won't believe how cool it is!

"The power under the Constitution will always be with the people."

—*George Washington*

This portrait of George Washington, painted in 1796, is displayed at the National Portrait Gallery.

ELIE WIESEL

SEPTEMBER 30, 1928–JULY 2, 2016

SURVIVOR OF THE HOLOCAUST
HUMANITARIAN
TEACHER
AUTHOR/PLAYWRIGHT
NOBEL PEACE PRIZE WINNER

Some really stupid people are saying the Holocaust never happened—but it did. Elie Wiesel knew it happened because he was there and he survived.

Have you ever heard of Auschwitz? It was a terrible place in Poland, one of the death camps (also known as concentration camps) where innocent people were slaughtered by the German Nazis during the 1940s. Elie Wiesel was only fifteen years old when he saw Nazi soldiers lead his mother and younger sister to their deaths in an Auschwitz gas chamber. Later, at another death camp called Buchenwald, he watched his father die of hunger and disease.

Following the defeat of the Nazis in 1945 and the world's discovery of the horrors of the death camps, sixteen-year-old Elie was taken to France. Try to imagine how he felt. He was now an orphan. He had witnessed incredible scenes of brutality and torture on a daily basis. He had felt the gut-wrenching pangs of hunger and had been beaten when camp guards were mad at him. He had worked daily surrounded by fellow Jews who were sick and dying. And he bore a number—A17713—that the Nazis had tattooed on him, so that they could strip him of his name along with his human dignity. So many of the people who had been part of young Elie's life were gone. His parents—gone. His neighbors and friends from his small village

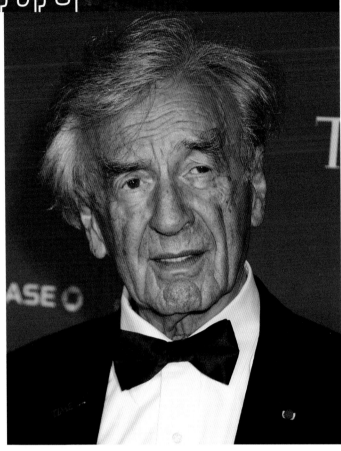

Elie Wiesel has been honored with numerous awards for his humanitarian work. In addition to the Nobel Peace Prize, he was awarded the United States Presidential Medal of Freedom. He is pictured here in 2012.

of Sighet in Transylvania—gone. His teachers who had praised his schoolwork—gone. And his rabbi, who for his bar mitzvah had taught him the Torah—gone. Elie Wiesel's childhood had disappeared!

Miraculously, two of his sisters had also survived the death camps, and in France he was reunited with them. Strength came from having family back in his life. Determination came too, as he realized that he could not remain silent about what he had witnessed. He had vowed to say nothing for ten years. It was too painful to discuss what he had seen. But as reporters and historians started to reveal the magnitude

"Wherever men or women are persecuted because of their race, religion or political views, that place must—at that moment—become the center of the universe."

—*Elie Wiesel (from the speech he made when accepting the Nobel Peace Prize in 1986)*

DIVE IN!

Elie Wiesel: The Perils of Indifference by Rebecca Sjonger (Crabtree, 2021), 48 pages.

of the death camp horrors, Elie Wiesel began to see his life's mission. More than six million Jews and millions of others, and more than one and a half million of them children, were murdered in those death camps. Wiesel had lived through that horrible nightmare, that "hell on Earth." He knew that the world had to learn about and remember what had taken place there. And so he began to write and lecture about his experience as a survivor.

Through his work, Elie Wiesel became the voice for the Holocaust. That's what he called the mass murder by the Nazis, and it is the label the world now uses to identify that horrendous ordeal. In the Greek language, the word *holocaust* means, "a sacrifice burned in its entirety." Millions of adults and children were all sacrificed, and Elie Wiesel wanted to prevent it from ever happening again.

In 1963 he became a US citizen, having moved to New York City to continue his speaking and writing. It had been US soldiers who nearly twenty years earlier had set him free.

Spared a torturous death in his youth, Elie Wiesel has worked hard to promote world peace and human rights. His more than fifty books have made him a world-famous author.

In 1986 Wiesel received the Nobel Peace Prize in recognition of his efforts to make our world a safer, more loving place. He used his prize money of $290,000 to establish the Elie Wiesel Foundation for Humanity (www.eliewieselfoundation.org), an organization that promotes the elimination of hate and intolerance. Until his death, Elie Wiesel continued to work for peace and promoted human rights throughout the world.

EXPLORE!

The United States Holocaust Memorial Museum opened in 1993 to honor the Holocaust's victims. The museum was built to help us remember, learn, and keep this genocide from happening again. Read Elie Wiesel's Power Words. Can we afford to forget the Holocaust? If we do, who will be the next victims? Your neighbor? Your teacher? Your family? You? We must remember.

Explore the United States Holocaust Memorial Museum at www.ushmm.org. Maybe you can visit the museum in person someday too. Remember . . . and learn.

OPRAH WINFREY

JANUARY 29, 1954–

MEDIA ICON
BUSINESSPERSON
HUMANITARIAN
ACTIVIST
ACTOR
AUTHOR

O! She might be the only famous person in the United States who can be easily identified by a single letter. Oprah Winfrey is one of the most successful, talented, charismatic, and strong-willed, people in the world. She had a remarkable journey from a poor rural Mississippi upbringing to become the richest Black person of the twentieth century, according to *Forbes* magazine. It is a story of hard work, determination, and superhuman perseverance.

Oprah's childhood was tough. Born to a teenage mother with little money, the family struggled to get by. Oprah wore clothes made of potato sacks to save money. She was sometimes bullied, abused, and beaten by relatives.

Through it all, Oprah proved she could survive tough times and thrive. Education was her way to escape the chains of poverty. Having learned to read by the time she was three years old, thanks to her grandmother, Oprah knew the joy of escaping into a book.

Winfrey's affinity for language started her down a career path, first as a radio and TV reporter and then as a TV talk show host. Over the years *The Oprah Winfrey Show* became more and more popular. She branched out

The Oprah Winfrey Show **ran on television for twenty-five seasons, from 1986 to 2011. After ending the show, Winfrey went on to other ventures in TV, movies, publishing, and much more. She even started her own television network called the Oprah Winfrey Network.**

into acting, writing, publishing, and other ventures.

Winfrey built a media empire and became incredibly wealthy. But she has goals that are more far-reaching than getting rich, and a school in South Africa knows exactly how far-reaching they are. She founded the Oprah Winfrey Leadership Academy for Girls in 2007. Knowing firsthand the power of education, Winfrey is determined to provide learning opportunities for girls and young women in South Africa. From 1948 to the early 1990s, Black people in South Africa were separated from whites under a cruel legal system known as apartheid. Winfrey's school seeks to give

students a first-rate education so they can improve the quality of their lives and leave the horrors of apartheid behind.

Winfrey interviews actor Elliot Page in April 2021. At the time, Page was in the process of a gender transition, which he discussed with Winfrey.

EXPLORE!

Ever heard of the Oprah effect? The phrase is used to describe how popular a book can become if Winfrey chooses it as one of her book club selections.

Oprah's Book Club was born in 1996. Winfrey chose a book and asked her fans to read it. When she later discussed the book on her show, viewers could take part in the discussion. Books had been an important part of Winfrey's life from a very young age, and the book club allowed her to share her passion with millions of people. The books Winfrey chooses instantly become popular, and sales soar. That's the Oprah effect!

Now it's your turn. We want YOU to create the hero effect. Read the Dive In! sidebars in this book for further reading inspiration for each of the 60 heroes. We want you to dive in, read some of those books, and write brief reviews. Did you like a book? Tell us why! Be sure to be honest. If you weren't crazy about a book, you can tell us that too. Do you think other kids should read the book? Is so, spread the word. That's the hero effect!

Go to our website, www.heroes4us.com, and click on "Contact" in the upper-right part of the screen. Fill in your name and e-mail address, paste your book review into the Message box, then click Submit. Our goal is to encourage readers to learn a lot more about the heroes in this book.

Thank you, Oprah Winfrey, for encouraging all of us to read—and thank YOU for helping to create the hero effect!

POWER WORDS!

"It doesn't matter who you are, where you come from. The ability to triumph begins with you. Always, always." —*Oprah Winfrey*

WILBUR AND ORVILLE WRIGHT

WILBUR:
APRIL 16, 1867–MAY 30, 1912

ORVILLE:
AUGUST 19, 1871–JANUARY 30, 1948

THE FIRST MEN TO FLY
INVENTORS
AVIATORS
AUTHORS

This photo of Wilbur *(left)* and Orville Wright was published in 1909.

Count 1,001, 1,002, 1,003, 1,004, 1,005, 1,006, 1,007, 1,008, 1,009, 1,010, 1,011, 1,012. That's twelve seconds. That's how long the historic first airplane flight lasted. Just twelve seconds. The plane flew 120 feet (37 m), not even half a football field. But it was enough to prove that humans could fly. Two brothers, Orville and Wilbur Wright, designed and built the motor-driven machine that picked them up off the ground on December 17, 1903, and sent them soaring into the history books. What led the Wright brothers to that historic event on the beach at Kitty Hawk, North Carolina? Well, believe it or not, it was a bicycle.

Ten years earlier, Wilbur and Orville Wright had opened a bicycle repair shop in Ohio. They then began designing new bicycles. Their success in building lightweight bikes, combined with their fascination with gliders (aircraft with no engines), led them to a new interest: flying.

When they were children, their father surprised them once with a toy helicopter. It was made of cork, bamboo, and paper, and powered by a rubber band. They loved playing with it and used it as a model to make their own. Years later, the Wright brothers claimed that their toy helicopter contributed to their interest in flying. Their first experiments with flight involved nonpowered machines called gliders.

They spent years learning the principles of flight before they moved on to powered aircraft. Then there were more years of study and experimentation, until Orville Wright piloted that historic twelve-second flight, with Wilbur Wright running alongside the airplane. Three more flights took place that morning, with the brothers taking turns at the controls. The longest flight of the day was 852 feet (260 m) and lasted fifty-nine seconds. Wilbur Wright was in the pilot's seat.

Then the brothers became rich and famous, right? Wrong! The world didn't even hear about what they'd done for another five years. Want to know why? You'll have to read their story to find out!

EXPLORE!

In 2003 we celebrated the one-hundredth anniversary of the Wright brothers' first flight. Explore the history, the machines, and the people who have gone "up, up and away" since that December day in 1903.

There are lots of ways to learn more about

DIVE IN!

Race through the Skies: The Week the World Learned to Fly by Martin W. Sandler (Bloomsbury Children's Books, 2020), 185 pages.

The Wright Brothers by Lewis Helfand (Kalyani Navyug Media, 2011), 68 pages.

flying and aviators. Start by exploring the Smithsonian National Air and Space Museum at www.airandspace.si.edu. In addition to learning about the history of aviation, you'll find all the latest flying news there. The Wright Brothers National Memorial in North Carolina is a must-see for fans of human flight. Find out more about the park at www.nps.gov/wrbr.

We want you to think about this question: Of all of the great inventions in the history of humankind, is the airplane THE greatest? If not, what is? Let us know, and we'll compile the list once we receive enough messages. Do you have an idea for an invention that will change the world? Tell us about that too!

POWER WORDS!

"I cannot but believe that we stand at the beginning of a new era, The Age of Flight." —*Orville Wright*

One of the earliest airplanes designed by Wilbur and Orville Wright glides above the ground. It was not only their knowledge of aerodynamics but also their skill as pilots that contributed to their eventual success.

LOUIS ZAMPERINI

JANUARY 26, 1917–JULY 2, 2014

GREATEST GENERATION SUPERSTAR
WORLD WAR II VETERAN AND PRISONER OF WAR
INSPIRATIONAL WRITER AND SPEAKER
OLYMPIC ATHLETE

Louis Zamperini competed for the University of Southern California in the late 1930s.

How much pain can a person endure? Thankfully most of us will never know the answer to that question. But Louis Zamperini knew.

When Zamperini was very young, he was best known for getting into trouble. But in high school, he started getting attention for his running ability. He became one of Southern California's top athletes. At the age of nineteen, Zamperini was the youngest athlete to compete in the 1936 Olympic Games. That year the Olympics were held in Berlin, Germany, where Adolf Hitler and the Nazis were growing in power. Zamperini didn't win a medal. He hoped to do better at the 1940 Olympic Games, but they were canceled due to World War II.

Zamperini joined the US Army Air Corps. He enlisted in 1941, shortly before the United States entered the war. He became a bombardier and flew missions over the Pacific Ocean. While on a mission to find a missing pilot in 1943, his plane crashed due to engine failure. Of the eleven-person crew, only Zamperini and two others survived.

Stranded on the ocean in a life raft, Zamperini, Francis McNamara, and Russell Allen Phillips faced incredible pain. It came from the sun. It came from hunger and thirst. They were terrorized from below by sharks circling their raft and from above by the bombs and guns of Japanese airplanes.

POWER WORDS!

"The one who forgives never brings up the past to that person's face. When you forgive, it's like it never happened. True forgiveness is complete and total."

—*Louis Zamperini*

Zamperini and his companions struggled with pain and terror night and day. With little water or food, the men were weak, and McNamara died. Finally, after forty-seven days at sea, Zamperini and Phillips washed ashore almost 2,000 miles (3,219 km) from where their plane had crashed.

Zamperini and Phillips had landed on an island controlled by the enemy, and they were soon taken prisoner by Japanese forces. Then they would know a new kind of pain. Because Zamperini was an officer and a famous athlete, his captors hurt him the most.

This time, the pain came from brutal torture at the hands of a camp officer known as the Bird. It came from imprisonment in a small isolation cell. It came from hunger. It came twenty-four hours a day for more than two years—and Zamperini survived.

How did he do it? How did he survive pain that many would find impossible to endure? By praying and having faith. And by being determined to finish every race he ever ran.

During his time as a prisoner, Zamperini was officially declared dead by the US military. But he returned as a hero to the country he loved after the war. Zamperini had faced immeasurable pain, and he had endured!

EXPLORE!

When Laura Hillenbrand first heard about Louis Zamperini, she just had to tell the world his story. And that's what she did when she wrote the book *Unbroken: A World War II Story of Survival, Resilience, and Redemption*. After reading the book, famed actor Angelina Jolie was so inspired that she directed a 2014 movie about Zamperini's tale, also called *Unbroken*. Watch the movie with an adult, but be sure to keep some tissues handy—it might make you cry. You'll learn how Zamperini came to forgive those who had tortured him—even the Bird. Zamperini's story conveys a powerful message about faith and overcoming mental pain through forgiveness.

This photo of Louis Zamperini was taken in Los Angeles in 2011. He lived to the age of ninety-seven.

DIVE IN!

Unbroken: An Olympian's Journey from Airman to Castaway to Captive by Laura Hillenbrand (Random House Children's Books, 2017), 320 pages.

EXPLORE SOME MORE!

So many stories of courage that members of the Greatest Generation lived through aren't known because they were never recorded. Who belongs to the Greatest Generation? People born between 1900 and 1920, who were teens and adults during World War II.

You can help find and tell more stories like Zamperini's before they are lost completely. Search in your family and in your community for people who served in World War II and talk to them. Write down their stories. Several national efforts are under way to tell and preserve stories like these. Explore the Veterans History Project (https://loc.gov/vets), an organization that is dedicated to preserving the stories of our brave veterans.

EVEN MORE AMERICAN HEROES!

American history has far too many heroes to include all of them in this book. Read on to learn about ten people who just missed the cut. Then search online to find out even more about these great Americans.

LOUIS ARMSTRONG
AUGUST 4, 1901–JULY 6, 1971
THE KING OF JAZZ
SINGER AND TRUMPET PLAYER

No musician influenced jazz more than Louis Armstrong. Fans around the world instantly recognized his trumpet playing and gravelly singing voice. Armstrong was beloved by fans because they recognized his extraordinary musical ability and his commitment to equal treatment for all Americans. Explore Armstrong's life as a musician and US civil rights icon at https://www.louisarmstronghouse.org/biography/.

KEN BURNS
JULY 29, 1953–
THE MASTER OF DOCUMENTARY FILMS
MOVIEMAKER

In many ways, Ken Burns is one of America's greatest teachers. His films bring history to life. Through amazing photographs, videos, and music, a Ken Burns documentary captivates its viewers. His films cover a wide range of topics, from the US Civil War to baseball to country music. All of his films entertain and educate. Visit https://pbslearningmedia.org/collection/kenburnsclassroom/home/ to learn more about them.

MARY CASSATT
MAY 22, 1844–JANUARY 14, 1926
AMERICA'S GREAT IMPRESSIONIST
ARTIST

Art history includes many male impressionist painters, but the United States has the most famous female artist in this style! Mary Cassatt's paintings are in many major world art museums, and as a woman in a field dominated by men, she had to work extra hard for acceptance. Visit this website to learn more about her story and view some of her paintings: https://kids.kiddle.co/Mary_Cassatt.

MARTHA GRAHAM
MAY 11, 1894–APRIL 1, 1991
A REVOLUTIONARY IN DANCE
DANCER AND CHOREOGRAPHER

Martha Graham knew that she didn't dance the way other dancers did, and that was fine with her. She brought an entirely new vision to the world of dance, and her freedom of movement and emotional energy still affects how people dance! Find out more about her at https://kids.britannica.com/kids/article/Martha-Graham/390788.

MATTHEW HENSON
AUGUST 8, 1866–MARCH 9, 1955
THE MAN ON TOP OF THE WORLD
EXPLORER AND ADVENTURER

In 1909 Matthew Henson played a huge role in the first successful expedition to the North Pole. But because he was Black, he didn't receive the recognition he deserved. The difficult thirty-six-day journey was a success largely because of Henson's skills, and the famous mission entered the history books. Explore his life and adventures at https://kids.britannica.com/kids/article/Matthew-Henson/399967.

JACKIE JOYNER-KERSEE
MARCH 3, 1962–
OLYMPIC CHAMPION
ATHLETE AND HUMANITARIAN

Named by *Sports Illustrated* as the twentieth century's best female athlete, Jackie Joyner-Kersee competed in the grueling heptathlon—a competition made up of seven challenging track-and-field events. She won the heptathlon gold medal in two consecutive Olympics! Off the field, she has helped kids through the Jackie Joyner-Kersee Foundation. Learn more at https://jjkfoundation.org/.

CHRISTOPHER REEVE
SEPTEMBER 25, 1952–OCTOBER 10, 2004
SUPERMAN
ACTIVIST, ACTOR, AND DIRECTOR

When actor Christopher Reeve starred in action-packed Superman movies, he could fly. But after a horseback riding accident in 1995, he was permanently paralyzed below his neck. Through courage and perseverance, Reeve became a true superman as he supported research to help cure spinal cord injuries. Read about his life and career at https://www.christopherreeve.org/about-us/christopher -and-dana/christopher-reeve.

CAL RIPKEN JR.
AUGUST 24, 1960–
IRON MAN
ATHLETE AND HUMANITARIAN

Cal Ripken Jr. set a sports record that may never be broken. Baseball's Iron Man never missed a game in sixteen years as a professional player. For 2,632 straight games, he put on his Baltimore Orioles uniform and played ball. Just like the superathlete he was, Ripken Jr. is a superstar off the field by promoting literacy for adults. Discover other ways he and his family help their community at https://www.ripkenfoundation.org/.

ROY ROGERS AND DALE EVANS
ROGERS: NOVEMBER 5, 1911–JULY 6, 1998
EVANS: OCTOBER 31, 1912–FEBRUARY 7, 2001
KING OF THE COWBOYS AND QUEEN OF THE WEST
HUMANITARIANS
MOVIE STARS
SINGERS

Fans adored Roy Rogers and Dale Evans for more than their acting and singing talents. The extraordinary performers were beloved for their charity work and the attention they paid to abused and neglected children. Their commitment to each other and to their values was heroic. Read about their lives, careers, and much more at https://www.happytrails.org/index.htm.

IDA B. WELLS
JULY 16, 1862–MARCH 25, 1931
ANTI-LYNCHING CRUSADER
JOURNALIST AND HUMANITARIAN

After the US Civil War, Ida B. Wells knew that thousands of Black people in the South were lynched, or illegally hanged by mobs. She fought the violence through the power of her writing, and her words helped awaken people's minds and hearts to the plight of Black people. Find out how she did it at https://kids.nationalgeographic.com/history/article/ida-b-wells.

We are sure we missed someone YOU think is a hero.
Tell us who that person is! Why do you think that individual is a REAL hero? Let us know at www.heroes4us.com, and maybe your hero will be in the next edition of this book!

HERO HUNT

We want to challenge you! Too often, authors think they have to tell you everything. Well, we know that you can track down even more interesting stories of real heroes on your own if we provide a "trail." So, get your computer ready or head to the library and start hunting!

All the new heroes you will discover have some connection with one of our 60. Think about the links, and if a particular hero sparks your curiosity, search for connections to even more heroes.

It's not a contest, but we would love to know how many heroes you found before you turned to the answers on page 142. Send us a message at the website found in this book's introduction. Happy Hunting!

1. **(Susan B. Anthony, p. 12)** Susan B. Anthony is sort of the MVP of the All-Star team of suffragettes. You'll learn about some of the other team members by researching people like Elizabeth Cady Stanton and Lucretia Mott. But there's an earlier champion of woman's rights in our country. During the founding days of our new nation, she continually reminded her husband of the importance of equal rights for women. He listened but didn't break from the traditions of the times. Who is this woman? Hint: She became our second First Lady.

2. **(Clara Barton, p. 14)** Congress named this modern-day angel of a very different battlefield an honorary US citizen. Her "battlefields" were city slums in India, where she and her sisters provided care for the poorest of the poor. Who is this remarkable person?

3. **(Elizabeth Blackwell, p. 18)** This accomplished Black surgeon also knew what it was like to struggle against prejudice while pursuing a dream. He crusaded for better medical care for Black people, counseled and assisted Black medical students, encouraged Black women to become nurses, and helped found one of the first interracial hospitals in the United States. Who is he?

4. **(Rachel Carson, p. 20)** We Americans love our cars, and we drive more of them than any nation in the world. But have all of our automobiles always been as safe as they should have been? One person didn't think so, and he wrote a book called *Unsafe at Any Speed* to get his message out to consumers and car manufacturers. And he was successful. Who is he?

5. **(Jimmy Carter, p. 22)** Jimmy Carter learned about hard work, perseverance, and social justice from this amazing woman. She was a peanut farmer, a nurse, and a Peace Corps volunteer. She was also Jimmy Carter's mother! Who was she?

6. **(George Washington Carver, p. 24)** Dr. Carver worked with peanuts, but this famous scientist experimented with corn. Her parents did not want her to attend college, but she found a way to go. Genetics was her specialty. Who is she?

7. **(Walt Disney, p. 30)** This "dreamer's" characters are also a wonderful part of our popular culture. Some of you learned to count and to read with their help when you visited their "Street." A big bird named Big Bird became a favorite playmate of children everywhere. Who is this heroic artist?

8. **(Dwight D. Eisenhower, p. 42)** He was hailed as a true hero after the American Civil War as the Union general who had defeated the Confederacy after four long years of brutal war. Unfortunately, his eight years as president were not as successful. Still, upon his death in 1885, more than one million Americans witnessed his funeral procession. His tomb in New York is the largest mausoleum in North America. Who was he?

9. **(Benjamin Franklin, p. 46)** Sometimes known as "the other Benjamin," this hero was a free Black man in colonial America. Like Benjamin Franklin, this person was also an inventor, an astronomer, and a mathematician. Both men also wrote almanacs. Who was he?

10. **(John Glenn, p. 50)** He never flew in outer space. Yet he's called the Father of the US Space Program. He was the guiding force behind our efforts to explore the new frontier. His work with rockets, beginning in the 1920s, paved the way for astronauts walking on the moon. Who is he?

11. **(Amanda Gorman, p. 52)** Imagine a US president reading something you wrote! And not just any president, but the very first person to serve as our country's leader. George Washington read this poet's words in the eighteenth century. The writer was an enslaved person, and her poems were published in England and New England. Can you name her?

12. **(Kamala Harris, p. 54)** When Kamala Harris became the first Black woman to be elected US vice president, she knew that other distinguished women had bravely paved the way for her. Among them was this trailblazer, the first Black woman in Congress and the first Black woman to seek the nomination for US president from one of the two major political parties. Her campaign motto was "unbought and unbossed." Who was she

13. **(Milton Hershey, p. 58)** Just like Milton Hershey, this woman saved her hard-earned money and then gave a lot of it away to help others, but she was not a business owner like Hershey. She washed other people's clothes for a living. She saved a portion of her earnings for many years, and when she retired, she donated $150,000 to the University of Southern Mississippi to use for scholarships for Black students. Who was this hardworking and generous woman who proved that one person CAN make a difference?

14. **(Team Hoyt, p. 60)** Although a 1967 diving accident left her without the use of her legs or hands, this woman is an author, artist, and advocate for the disabled. During her term on the National Council on Disability, the Americans with Disabilities Act became law. She has received many awards and honorary degrees for her work. Who is she?

15. **(Helen Keller and Anne Sullivan, p. 68)** A very famous inventor was a good friend of Helen's parents. This man recommended Annie Sullivan as the teacher who could help young Helen. All his life he hoped his inventions would benefit people with hearing problems. Who is he?

16. **(John Muir, p. 80)** Many kids think he wasn't real. You've probably read folktales about the man who traveled around many parts of the eastern United States planting apple trees. Wearing his cooking pot as his hat, Johnny Appleseed became a familiar sight to frontier settlers. Read about one of our first conservationists and answer this question: What was his real name?

17. **(Jesse Owens, p. 86)** As a child, her legs were affected by the terrible disease polio. But by the age of eight she had learned how to walk. Then she learned to run. She was the first American woman to win three Olympic gold medals in running events. Who is she?

18. **(I. M. Pei, p. 94)** Another Asian American designed a very special monument found in our nation's capital. The simple "Wall" has the names of all Americans killed in the Vietnam War (1957–1975). Who designed this beloved memorial?

19. **(Theodore Roosevelt, p. 106)** In 1906 Theodore Roosevelt signed the Meat Inspection Act. The law ensures that meat and meat products are processed under clean and humane conditions. This man's 1905 novel, *The Jungle*, showed that we needed this law. His book described dangerous working conditions and unsanitary practices in the meat industry. If you eat meat, thank the author of *The Jungle*. What is his name?

20. **(Jonas Salk, p. 108)** About one hundred years ago, a terrible disease called yellow fever killed many people. A famous medical researcher dedicated his life to finding its cause and did so. A major research hospital in our nation's capital is named in his honor. Who is he?

21. **(Tecumseh, p. 112)** Almost none of the Native American nations had a written language. Their cultures used only the spoken word. One brilliant Cherokee, with the help of his equally intelligent daughter, developed an alphabet for his nation. Who is this father-daughter team?

22. **(Elie Wiesel, p. 122)** He personally saved over fifty thousand people from being killed during the Holocaust. He wasn't a US citizen, but Congress believed he was so special that they made him an Honorary American (one of only eight people in history so honored). Note the address of the Holocaust Museum.

23. **(Oprah Winfrey, p. 124)** On Easter Sunday in 1939, she performed one of the most important concerts in US history on the steps of the Lincoln Memorial in the nation's capital. This Black woman's amazing operatic voice, poise, and joy helped show how wrong racial segregation was. Who is she? (Once you learn who she is, find the concert online and listen for yourself to a thrilling moment in American history.)

24. **(Wright brothers, p. 126)** The story of aviation is full of fascinating and courageous heroes. Among them are Charles Lindbergh and Amelia Earhart, whose solo flights earned them a place in history. (What do you mean you never heard of them? Well go look them up!) Anyway, the famous aviator we have in mind became the first to break the sound barrier. Today lots of jets fly faster than the speed of sound, but this pioneering pilot was the first to push his plane into sonic boom territory. Who is he?

POWER WORDS SOURCES

JANE ADDAMS
"Political Reform" in *Democracy and Social Ethics* by Jane Addams, 1902

SUSAN B. ANTHONY
speech: "Woman's Rights to the Suffrage," 1873, Rochester, NY

CLARA BARTON
letter to Annie Childs, May 28, 1863, found in *The Life of Clara Barton* by William Barton, vol. 1, AMS Press, 1969, reprinted from 1922. Entire text of letter, pp. 221–224

MARY MCLEOD BETHUNE
"My Last Will and Testament" by Mary McLeod Bethune, originally published in *Ebony*, August 1955

ELIZABETH BLACKWELL
Medicine as a Profession for Women by Elizabeth Blackwell with Emily Blackwell, 1860

RACHEL CARSON
Silent Spring by Rachel Carson, 1962

JIMMY CARTER
American Heroes: Their Lives, Their Values, Their Beliefs by Robert B. Pamplin Jr. and Gary K. Eisler (Master Media Ltd., 1995), p. 13. Based on a first-person interview

GEORGE WASHINGTON CARVER
letter to Booker T. Washington from Carver discussing Carver's appointment to Tuskegee Institute faculty, April 12, 1896

CESAR CHAVEZ AND DOLORES HUERTA
Chavez—Cesar E. Chavez Foundation
Huerta—interview with Dolores Huerta, quoted in *With These Hands: Women Working on the Land* by Joan M. Jensen (McGraw-Hill Book Co., 1981)

ROBERTO CLEMENTE
speech before the Baseball Writers of Houston, Texas, 1971

WALT DISNEY
Preface to Walt Disney World (Walt Disney Company, 1986), p. 2

DOROTHEA DIX
Encyclopedia of Women Social Reformers: Volume One (ABC-CLIO, 2001), p. 199

FREDERICK DOUGLASS
speech at civil rights mass meeting, Washington, DC, October 22, 1883

MARIAN WRIGHT EDELMAN
quoted in *Time* magazine, March 1987

THOMAS EDISON
said circa 1903, quoted in *Harper's Monthly Magazine*, September 1932

ALBERT EINSTEIN
The Quotable Einstein collected and edited by Alice Calaprice (Princeton University Press, 1996), p. 223 (quote attributed to Einstein)

DWIGHT D. EISENHOWER
Order of the Day, June 6, 1944, a message to the troops before D-day

ANTHONY FAUCI
from an interview with CNN, May 2020

BENJAMIN FRANKLIN
in a letter to B. Vaughan, March 14, 1743

RUTH BADER GINSBURG
from a speech given at the Harvard Radcliffe Institute, June 2015

JOHN GLENN
address to joint session of US Congress, February 26, 1962
John Glenn: A Memoir by John Glenn with Nick Taylor (Bantam Books, 1999), p. 404

AMANDA GORMAN
from the poem "The Hill We Climb," recited at the US presidential inauguration, January 2021

KAMALA HARRIS
from her victory speech after the 2020 US presidential election

JOHN HERRINGTON
from a speech given at Naval Air Systems Command, November 2020

MILTON HERSHEY
An Intimate Story of Milton S. Hershey by Joseph Richard Snavely (J. Horace McFarland Co., 1957)

TEAM HOYT
Rick Hoyt, 1977, later posted on www.teamhoyt.com

LANGSTON HUGHES
from *The Dream Keeper and Other Poems*, 1932

THOMAS JEFFERSON
Declaration of Independence

KATHERINE JOHNSON
Reaching for the Moon: The Autobiography of NASA Mathematician Katherine Johnson by Katherine Johnson (Atheneum Books for Young Readers, 2019), 88.

HELEN KELLER
The Story of My Life, 1902, Chapter 4

THE REVEREND DR. MARTIN LUTHER KING JR.
Strength to Love by Martin Luther King Jr. (Harper & Row, 1963)

LEWIS, CLARK, AND SACAGAWEA
The Corps of Discovery, 1805

ABRAHAM LINCOLN
Gettysburg Address

YO-YO MA
from an interview "Yo-Yo Ma and the Meaning of Life," *New York Times*, https://www.nytimes.com/interactive/2020/11/23/magazine/yo-yo-ma-interview.html

GEORGE C. MARSHALL
lecture, Oslo University, January 1, 1954

JOHN MUIR
quoted by John T. Nicholas in *National History* magazine, November 1992

BARACK OBAMA
New Hampshire primary speech, January 8, 2008

SANDRA DAY O'CONNOR
from *Equal Justice: A Biography of Sandra Day O'Connor* by Harold and Geraldine Woods (Dillon Press, 1985)

JESSE OWENS
Jesse, A Spiritual Autobiography by Jesse Owens and Paul Neimark (Logos International, 1978)

ROSA PARKS
from *I Am Rosa Parks* by Rosa Parks with Jim Haskins (Dial Books for Young Readers, 1997), p. 28

DOLLY PARTON
posted on Twitter, February 2015

WALTER PAYTON
Never Die Easy: The Autobiography of Walter Payton by Walter Payton and Don Yaeger (Villard, 2000), 179.

I. M. PEI
from an interview "Wow! Perhaps I'm Not So Ancient After All," *Guardian*, https://www.theguardian.com/artanddesign/2010/feb/28/im-pei-architecture-interview

RONALD REAGAN
speech at the Brandenburg Gate in Berlin, Germany, June 12, 1987

JACKIE ROBINSON AND BRANCH RICKEY
Robinson—*I Never Had It Made: An Autobiography* by Jackie Robinson as told to Alfred Duckett (Ecco Press, 1995)
Rickey—"Rickey Should Be Remembered," by Bob Nightengale, April 2, 1997, http://www.sportingnews.com

FRED ROGERS
from an interview with Karen Herman, July 1999

ELEANOR ROOSEVELT
quoted in *Catholic Digest*, August 1960, p. 102

FRANKLIN ROOSEVELT
First Inaugural Address, March 4, 1933, *Public Papers*, vol. 2, 1938, p. 11

THEODORE ROOSEVELT
from a speech given in the Dakota Territory, July 4, 1886

JONAS SALK
quoted while accepting a special citation from President Dwight Eisenhower at the White House, April 22, 1955

ALEXANDRA SCOTT
quoted from a message on www.alexslemonade.org

TECUMSEH
Council at Vincennes, Indiana Territory, August 14, 1810. Tecumseh was responding to request that he sit at "his father's" (Governor William Henry Harrison's) side

HARRY S. TRUMAN
from *Plain Speaking: An Oral Biography of Harry S. Truman* by Merle Miller (Berkley Publishing Corp., 1973)

HARRIET TUBMAN
words carved into a plaque hanging in the Cayuga County (New York) Courthouse. Photograph of plaque is found in *Freedom Train* by Dorothy Sterling (Doubleday & Co. Inc., 1954)

MADAM C. J. WALKER
from a speech given at a business convention, 1917

GEORGE WASHINGTON
from a letter to Bushrod Washington, November 10, 1787

ELIE WIESEL
from Wiesel's acceptance speech, Nobel Peace Prize, Oslo, Norway, December 10, 1986

OPRAH WINFREY
"Oprah Winfrey on Courage," https://achievement.org/video/oprah-winfrey-11/

WRIGHT BROTHERS
Miracle at Kitty Hawk: The Letters of Wilbur and Orville Wright edited by Fred C. Kelly (Farrar, Straus & Young, 1951)

LOUIS ZAMPERINI
Devil at My Heels by Louis Zamperini and David Rensin (Morrow, 2003)

INDEX

ANSWERS TO HERO HUNT

ANSWERS

1. Abigail Adams
2. Mother Teresa
3. Daniel Hale Williams
4. Ralph Nader
5. Lillian Gordy Carter
6. Barbara McClintock
7. Jim Henson
8. Ulysses S. Grant
9. Benjamin Banneker
10. Robert Goddard
11. Phillis Wheatley
12. Shirley Chisholm
13. Osceola McCarty
14. Joni Eareckson Tada
15. Alexander Graham Bell
16. John Chapman
17. Wilma Rudolph
18. Maya Lin
19. Upton Sinclair
20. Dr. Walter Reed
21. Sequoyah and Ahyoka
22. Raoul Wallenberg
23. Marian Anderson
24. Chuck Yeager

PHOTO ACKNOWLEDGMENTS

Image credits: NASA, pp. 6 (top left), 50, 56, 57, 66; Wade Payne/Invision/AP, p. 6 (top right); Paul Natkin/Getty Images, p. 6 (middle left); NIAID/flickr (CC BY 2.0), pp. 6 (middle right), 44; PictureLux/The Hollywood Archive/Alamy Stock Photo, pp. 6 (bottom), 112; Library of Congress, pp. 10, 13, 14, 16, 22, 25, 34, 35, 38, 39, 40, 62, 68, 69, 70, 74, 78, 80, 81, 86, 100, 102, 103, 104, 105, 115, 126, 127, 131 (bottom); Wallace Kirkland/Photo Researchers History/Getty Images, p. 11; Everett Collection/Shutterstock.com, pp. 12, 83, 120; Peter Newark American Pictures/Bridgeman Images, p. 15; Afro American Newspapers/Gado/Getty Images, p. 17; Museum of the City of New York/Getty Images, p. 18; Interim Archives/Getty Images, p. 19; CBS Photo Archive/Getty Images, p. 20; AP Photo, pp. 21, 29, 31, 94, 101, 106, 107, 131 (middle), 133 (top); Charley Gallay/Getty Images, p. 23; Glasshouse Images/Alamy Stock Photo, p. 24; William Warren/Alamy Stock Photo, p. 26; Frank Hurley/NY Daily News Archive/Getty Images, p. 27; Focus On Sport/Getty Images, pp. 28, 92; Donaldson Collection/Getty Images, p. 30; National Portrait Gallery/Wikimedia Commons, pp. 32, 47; AP Photo/Gerry Broome, p. 33; Cynthia Johnson/Getty Images, p. 36; AP Photo/Rogelio V. Solis, p. 37; National Archives, pp. 41, 79; Popperfoto/Getty Images, p. 42; White Houses/Wikimedia Commons, p. 43; AP Photo/Patrick Semansky, Pool, pp. 45, 53; Gift of Mrs. W. Murray Crane/National Gallery of Art, Washington DC, p. 46; Steve Petteway/Supreme Court of the United States/Wikimedia Commons, p. 48; LBJ Foundation Photo/Jay Godwin/flickr, p. 49; Joseph Sohm/Shutterstock.com, pp. 51, 82; AP Photo/Richard Shotwell/Invision, p. 52; Official White House Photo by Lawrence Jackson, p. 54; DoD photo by U.S. Air Force Senior Airman Kevin Tanenbaum/flickr, p. 55; Underwood Archives/Getty Images, pp. 58, 114; Everett Collection Historical/Alamy Stock Photo, p. 59; AP Photo/Tom DiPace, pp. 60, 61; Hulton Archive/Getty Images, p. 63; Gift of Thomas Jefferson Coolidge IV in memory of his great-grandfather, Thomas Jefferson Coolidge, his grandfather, Thomas Jefferson Coolidge II, and his father, Thomas Jefferson Coolidge III/National Gallery of Art, Washington DC, p. 64; Ron Sachs/CNP/dpa picture alliance/Alamy Stock Photo, p. 67; Arnie Sachs/CNP/dpa picture alliance/Alamy Stock Photo, p. 71; Independence National Historical Park, p. 72; Todd Strand/Independent Picture Service, p. 73; Gregory F. Maxwell/Wikimedia Commons (GFDL-1.2), p. 75; AP Photo/Robert E. Klein, p. 76; Tom Williams/CQ Roll Call/Getty Images, p. 77; Mark Wilson/Getty Images, p. 84; Joel Shawn/Shutterstock.com, p. 85; Bettmann/Getty Images, pp. 87, 88, 98, 117; AP Photo/Gene Herrick, p. 89; AP Photo/Rob Carr, p. 90; © Jim Stevens/flickr, p. 91; AP Photo/Bruce Zake, p. 93; Erdal Akan/Shutterstock.com, p. 95; Wikimedia Commons (public domain), pp. 96, 133 (bottom); AP Photo/Ira Schwartz, p. 97; AP Photo/Harry Harris, p. 99; Courtesy of Alexslemonade.org, pp. 108, 109; MPI/Archive Photos/Getty Images, p. 110; Internet Archive Book Images/Wikimedia Commons, p. 111; AP Photo/Gene J. Puskar, p. 113; Collection of the National Museum of African American History and Culture shared with the Library of Congress, p. 116; Smithsonian Institution, National Museum of American History/Wikimedia Commons, p. 118; Collection of the Smithsonian National Museum of African American History and Culture, Gift from Dawn Simon Spears and Alvin Spears, Sr., p. 119; National Portrait Gallery, Smithsonian Institution; acquired as a gift to the nation through the generosity of the Donald W. Reynolds Foundation, p. 121; Nancy Kaszerman/ZUMA Press, Inc./Alamy Stock Photo, p. 122; Joe Seer/Shutterstock.com, p. 124; AP Photo/EMPPL PA Wire, p. 125; Photo by Louis Zamperini/Bob Riha, Jr./Archive Photos/Getty Images, p. 128; Noel Vasquez/Getty Images, p. 129; AP Photo/Virginian-Pilot, Perry Breon, p. 130 (top); Shawn Miller/Library of Congress/flickr (CC0 1.0), p. 130 (bottom); CSU Archives/Everett Collection/Alamy Stock Photo, p. 131 (top); AP Photo/Lennox Mclendon, p. 132 (top); AP Photo/Ron Edmonds, p. 132 (middle); AP Photo/Roberto Borea, p. 132 (bottom). Design element: NAimage/iStock/Getty Images.

Cover: Jeffrey R. Staab/CBS via Getty Images (Yo-Yo Ma); PictureLux/The Hollywood Archive/Alamy Stock Photo (Fred Rogers); AP Photo/Rob Carr (Dolly Parton); DOD Photo by Navy Petty Officer 1st Class Carlos M. Vazquez II/flickr (CC BY 2.0) (Amanda Gorman); Library of Congress (Thomas Edison) (Abraham Lincoln) (Jesse Owens); NASA (John Herrington); Official White House Photo by Lawrence Jackson (Kamala Harris); Wikimedia Commons (public domain) (C.J. Walker); Bettmann/Getty Images (Rosa Parks); Mark Junge/Archive Photos/Getty Images (Cesar Chavez); Supreme Court of the United States/Steve Petteway/Wikimedia Commons (Ruth Bader Ginsburg); Nationaal Archief/Herbert Behrens/Anefo/Wikimedia Commons (CC0 1.0) (Louis Armstrong).

ABOUT THE AUTHORS

Dr. Dennis Denenberg is a nationally known speaker about REAL heroes and their importance to kids and adults. He has taken his message to forty-two states with the goal of presenting his lively presentation in all fifty! Visit www.heroes4us.com to see where he has been and where he still wants to speak.

A Phi Beta Kappa graduate of the College of William and Mary (where his hero, Thomas Jefferson, was formally educated), Dr. Denenberg obtained his doctorate from Pennsylvania State University. He taught high school social studies for six years, was an elementary school principal for five years, and was assistant superintendent of schools for four years. He finished his thirty-year career in education as a professor at Millersville University, where he taught future teachers how to make history and heroes come alive for kids. These days he writes a monthly feature called "Dr. D's Mystery Hero" for *Cobblestone* magazine.

In addition to his passion about REAL heroes, "Dr. D" loves to garden. In fact, his entire 1 acre (0.4 ha) property near Lancaster, Pennsylvania, is full of flower gardens—there's not a single blade of grass! Do you think the fact that Thomas Jefferson loved to garden had anything to do with this hobby?

His unsung personal heroes are his fantastic mom and dad, his speech teachers when he was young (he had a severe speech problem), and his eighth-grade history teacher, Alvin Hildebrand, who was also passionate about history. His other major unsung hero is his sister Diana, who battled breast cancer for eighteen years. He has started a foundation in her honor: Diana's Dreamers: Determined to Defeat Breast Cancer. Read about this group at www.heroes4us.com.

Lorraine Roscoe has been spreading the word about REAL heroes for more than twenty years. She has presented interactive programs to primary- and intermediate-age students, community groups, and college students. Through songs, anecdotes, games, props, and lots of audience participation, she tells stories of heroes profiled in *50 American Heroes Every Kid Should Meet*. Roscoe has shared her message at many schools and libraries as well as at the state conference of the Pennsylvania Association for Volunteerism. Roscoe has also presented workshops for preschool and early childhood educators seeking to incorporate the heroes concept into classrooms.

A graduate of Cabrini College in Radnor, Pennsylvania, Roscoe resides in Lancaster County, Pennsylvania, with her husband, Michael. Their family is important to them, including daughter Allison; her husband, Rich; and their son, Gavin, as well as daughter Bethany. Roscoe is currently community engagement manager for Power Packs Project, a nonprofit based in Lancaster, Pennsylvania.

Roscoe considers it a privilege to celebrate heroes with children and young people, and she applauds the parents, educators, and mentors who are doing the same.